Leading
hArtfully

WHAT PEOPLE ARE SAYING

"*Leading hArtfully* uplifts, inspires and provides a leadership pathway to discover the best in people. Laced with concrete, inspirational examples, it offers a clear framework for creating positive change and shows all of us how we can create 'change-a-world' moments. This book is a must-read for any leader committed to creating a culture where individuals thrive and flourish."

— MARY MARTUSCELLI, Regional President, US Bank

"In *Leading hArtfully*, Diane Rogers provides inspiration and practical steps for leading impactful positive change in the workplace. While written from a healthcare context, the framework is equally adaptable to any leadership setting, and her examples are easily relatable. Diane's 'before' story is told with a refreshing and searing honesty that invites leaders to look into the mirror of reflection on their own experiences. It is exciting to see the enormous 'change-a-world' ripple widening from Diane's first courageous choice to 'dive into the deep end' of trust with me as a volunteer client in coach training, spreading out through her coachees and the leaders who read her book, as they discover new ways of both being and doing that transform the workplace into centers of excellence and positive human spirit. I particularly appreciate the resonant value of her prompt to 'see the routine as remarkable,' coupled with a structured framework for 'holding up the mirror.'"

— LAURA R. ATWOOD, Master Certified Coach (MCC),
President of Adler Learning USA

"As a physician leader, I found Diane's stories and guidance to be a powerful tool in helping our organization build stronger teams through change. As a physician coached by Diane, I discovered the value in uncovering the best in others; she was instrumental in helping me to positively change my practice and patient interactions, and kick-started my journey to lead hArtfully. I highly recommend this book to physicians and leaders seeking to deliver exceptional quality care by magnificent individuals!"

— ALISON TOTHY, MD, Associate Professor of Pediatrics; Pediatric Emergency
Medicine, University of Chicago Medicine and Biological Sciences Division

"As you open the pages of *Leading hArtfully* and delve into the chapters, it's as if you are nestled in your favorite chair, with Diane alongside, embarking on your own adventure — uncovering a masterful compilation appealing to your head and heart simultaneously. *Leading hArtfully* has been a launching pad for significant cultural transformation within our organization. In recognizing the actions, attitudes and behaviors, and holding up the mirror to the magnificence within our teams, we are uncovering their best qualities that influence and impact patient care. *Leading hArtfully* is an energizing experience into possibility, which has additionally unlocked something much bigger within me. It forged a linkage where my logic and passion could work in harmony, thus changing not only my approach to work but to life as well."

— JANELL ROSS, **CPXP,** Patient Experience and Volunteer Services,
Garden City Hospital (Prime Healthcare)

"Diane Rogers makes me want to be a better person — a stronger, more people-centered leader and a business owner who never lets the 'work' get in the way of the wonder of human interaction. *Leading hArtfully* is like an executive coach in book form, full of humility and introspection... and difficult (but inspiring) epiphanies about the hard-driving leader I used to be and the 'hArtful' leader I aspire to be. Without doubt, the invitation to rethink my leadership style offered by Diane in this breakthrough book will reap results for everyone attached to my company. I envision improved business performance, reduced turnover, and motivated, engaged partners. And I am eager to practice her powerful method of accelerating and deepening individual engagement through her eight 'E's — enlighten, explode, energize, engage, encourage, experience, excite, and evolve. This book should be required reading for entrepreneurs and CEOs."

— KATE COLBERT, Market Research and Brand Consultant, Communications
Coach, Speaker, and Author of *Think Like a Marketer: How a Shift in Mindset
Can Change Everything for Your Business*

WHY YOU SHOULD READ THIS BOOK

If you have ever had the chance to meet Diane Rogers, you realize that you can feel her positive and enlivening presence before she even speaks a word. While presence may be something you would assume to be intangible, Diane has managed to capture its essence in this book, aptly titled *Leading hArtfully*. The idea that we can and MUST lead with heart is an even more essential need in today's world of disparate perspectives, expanding crises and hopefully positive social shifts.

Diane brings her own capacity to lead hArtfully to these pages through personal reflection and practical insights — all leading to clear and focused actions one can take for themselves or with others in elevating their capacity to contribute to and elevate the human experiences fostered at every point of interaction between people. In recognizing the importance of how you show up, to energizing with possibility, to the powerful idea of holding up the mirror, Diane challenges us to look both inward at our personal wiring and outward to our human connections to understand our personal capacity and our capability to positively impact others.

Perhaps that is the phrase that stuck with me most — *celebrating the capacity to change a world* — for that is what leading hArtfully can and will lead to overall. If you want to feel a sense of purpose brought to life and you want to experience passion in words that will inspire, that is the gift that Diane has given us here. Enjoy the ride.

—JASON A. WOLF, PhD, CPXP, President & CEO, The Beryl Institute

Leading
hArtfully

*The Art of Leading Through Your Heart
to Discover the Best in Others*

Diane M. Rogers

IGNITE
PRESS

Fresno, CA

Published in the United States by Ignite Press.
ignitepress.us

ISBN: 978-1-950710-60-7 (Amazon Print)
ISBN: 978-1-950710-61-4 (IngramSpark) PAPERBACK
ISBN: 978-1-950710-62-1 (IngramSpark) HARDCOVER
ISBN: 978-1-950710-63-8 (Smashwords)

For bulk purchase and for booking, contact:

Diane M. Rogers
www.contagiouschange.com

Library of Congress Control Number: 2020913430

Cover design by Shannon Slocum
Edited by Andrew Hirst
Publishing coordination by Malia Sexton

To my mom… the mold through which I emerged.

And, to the finest person in America, Jonrogers.
I am forever blessed to be your wife.

ACKNOWLEDGMENTS

"Discovery is an adventure that should always be shared."

- DIANE M. ROGERS

People often ask - "Why did you write a book"? And, consistently, the first response that pops into my head is - "Because I didn't think I could." Yes, surprisingly, that was my initial motivation, and yet, I obviously could (and did) write a book… but not without the help of some very key individuals.

Discovery IS an adventure that should always be shared…and with gobs of gratitude, I wish to acknowledge a few key individuals that have shared in my adventure of writing *Leading hArtfully*.

Cathy Fyock, Author, Book Coach
The Business Book Strategist
https://www.cathyfyock.com/

"Writing a book is like jumping out of an airplane.
The hardest part is making the leap…"

- CATHY FYOCK

Cathy Fyock is my book coach and the person who helped me take the leap into authorship. She is expert, encouraging and keenly intuitive, guiding me through the writing process and ever so graciously helping me to leverage my strengths and honor my commitments. She is a joy to work with, and (now) a very dear friend. I am ever so appreciative for her time, counsel and uplifting energy. If you are ready to take the leap into becoming an author, contact Cathy!

Shannon Slocum, Illustrator and Designer
Founder, Seriously Shannon
https://seriouslyshannon.com/

Shannon lights up every room she enters. Her delightful spirit and remarkable talent infuse her creativity, bringing to life concepts, models, and meaningful messages in ways that capture attention and invite engagement. She has this most amazing ability to inspire and motivate me through her designs, taking a half-baked idea and, through color, images and layout, turning it into a tangible, understandable, meaningful message. Shannon designed my book cover. Need I say more?

Lauren Gebhardt, Digital Social Media & Marketing Strategist
Geb Digital
https://www.gebdigital.com/

I vividly remember the first day I met Lauren. She was introduced to me as a marvelous bundle of social media expertise. And, while I can certainly echo this observation, what makes Lauren ever so remarkable is her enthusiasm and creativity in bringing alive stories, blogs, and lived experiences in meaningful, engaging ways. She is a magnet for hugs, and each time I meet with her, I leave feeling on top of the world. She has helped me to step into this new space of openness and sharing, in a comfortable, competent and confident way. Follow me on Twitter (@contagiouschang), LinkedIn (DianeMRogers) and Facebook (Contagious Change) and watch her magic unfold.

Editorial Review Board; Members

- *Jason Brown, MD* - Chief Medical Officer Pharmacy Services and Transfer Services, Banner Health

- *Deanna Frings* - Vice President, Learning & Professional Development, The Beryl Institute

- *Cathy Fyock* - Author, Book Coach, The Business Book Strategist

- *John Griffin* - Founder & CEO, Teamsmith

- *Sue Murphy*, RN BSN MS - Chief Experience Officer, Patient Experience and Engagement Program, University of Chicago Medicine

- *Bonni Scepkowski* - President & Chief Strategy Officer, Stellar Meetings and Events

- *Alison Tothy, MD* - Associate Professor of Pediatrics, Pediatric Emergency Medicine, University of Chicago Medicine

Each of these individuals was deeply immersed in the Leading hArtfully adventure. They were each invited to read the manuscript while in final draft form and to help bring forward, clearly and with meaning, the essence of leading through your heart. With an open mind and heart, they highlighted areas of magnificence, as well as those that needed further clarity, better transitions and additional details. I trusted each of them implicitly, knowing that they wanted the best for me, and for you, the reader. I paid attention to every single comment, incorporating their suggestions and acknowledging those things well done. At the end of this process, I not only had finalized a quality book, but could marvel in this incredible accomplishment. They helped me to feel profoundly proud of this book, and I am forever and deeply grateful.

Everett O'Keefe, Publisher
Ignite Press
https://www.ignitepress.us

Positive, respectful and energizing relationships are fundamental in choosing who I work with. So, it was no surprise that I would work with Everett after our initial meeting. He is thoughtful, thorough and patient, understanding that publishing a book is a personal and professional 'big deal'. He has the keen ability to nudge you forward in a way that feels incredibly supportive, acknowledging your progress and the big, bold, baby steps you are taking. Launching a book IS a really big deal… to me. And I am ever so grateful to have Everett's expertise and encouragement in bringing my book to print.

Kate Colbert, Founder and Principal Marketing Consultant
Silver Tree Communications
https://www.silvertreecommunications.com/

Have you ever met a person and you instantly knew there was chemistry between the two of you? Well, that was Kate and me. Our very first phone conversation created a powerful connection that took our personal and professional relationship to the next level. And that's exactly what she has done in helping to market my book. Kate is a word artist, taking my story, brand and coaching / consulting experience to the next level. Her business and marketing expertise is eloquently present in her work, and when coupled with her authentic, honest, and passionate support, help to create a collaborative, productive partnership. I feel fortunate to have made this connection and am confident it will be one that lasts a long time.

Significant & Formative Thought Leaders

- *Laura R. Atwood* - Certified Professional Coach (MCC), President, Adler Learning USA; https://lauraatwood.net

- *Marcus Buckingham* - New York Times best-selling author, researcher, and founder of the Strengths Revolution; https://www.marcusbuckingham.com/

- *Tim Gallwey* - Best-selling author of the Inner Game series of books, professional coach, and founder of The Inner Game; https://theinnergame.com/

- *Daniel Goleman* - New York Times best-selling author; Emotional Intelligence, Psychologist, and Science Journalist; http://www.danielgoleman.info/

- *Richard Leider* - Best-selling author, Executive Coach and Founder of Inventure - The Purpose Company; https://richardleider.com/

- *Catherine Morisset* - Certified Professional Coach (PCC), specializing in growing a thriving and resilient life; http://imagineplus.ca/

- *Ryan M. Niemiec*, Psy.D - Best-selling author, Psychologist, and Education Director, VIA Institute on Character; https://www.viacharacter.org/

- *Martin E. P. Seligman, Ph.D* - Best-selling author, Director of the Penn Positive Psychology Center and Zellerbach Family Professor of Psychology, University of Pennsylvania; https://ppc.sas.upenn.edu/people/martin-ep-seligman

TABLE OF CONTENTS

Foreword

Allow Me to Introduce You to Diane

I have been a nurse for more than 35 years and caring for patients has been the great privilege of my life. As the Chief Experience Officer at the University of Chicago Medicine, I've worked closely with a remarkable team of individuals who put heart and compassion at the core of creating exceptional human experiences, delivering quality, safe, reliable care to our patients and serving our community with humanity.

During my career as a leader and on the frontlines of healthcare, I have met many inspiring people. Among those people is Diane Rogers. Beyond being the president of Contagious Change® and the developer of The hArt of Medicine®, Diane is changing the world, along with making a difference every day.

I had the privilege of meeting Diane when a colleague introduced me to her after hearing her speak at a healthcare conference. She knew Diane's mission, vision and passion for improving the healthcare experience for all would resonate with me, and she was right. Diane's energy is contagious, and we connected immediately. Since our first conversation, we have been on a journey to strengthen and spread a culture of caring and excellence at UChicago Medicine.

As a certified professional coach, Diane helps people discover and optimize their strengths. As a caring human being, she believes every person has the capacity to drive positive change and impact in the lives of others. She sees the good in every person she meets, and she thrives on seeing people exceed their expectations. Over the years, I have been so impressed by the way Diane never falters in her mission to help others and manifest positive interactions. Day in and day out, she walks her talk.

The Book We've All Been Waiting For

And in this beautiful book, Diane helps others find their purpose and path so they, too, may walk their talk. She leads with her heart and teaches others to do the same. Always selfless, Diane shares personal experiences and professional journeys throughout this book to help others achieve their highest potential. Regardless of where you are in your career, there are valuable lessons to be learned. When I started reading the first few pages, it took me back to the first time I met Diane. Then and now, I recall a quote... "When the student is ready, the teacher appears." Diane was and is that teacher.

Diane also is a great storyteller. As you start reading her words, you will quickly realize that she speaks and leads from the heart. Throughout the book, Diane invites others to do the same and provides helpful tips along the way. Please note, you do not need to be a healthcare professional to have her words resonate. With each page, you will learn something valuable – no matter your livelihood or station in life. You also will discover that Diane, though perhaps a stranger, truly cares about you and helping you succeed. I hope you can feel the caring and hear the cheerleading in these pages. This book is a gift and so is Diane. So are you.

SUE MURPHY, RN BSN MS
Chief Experience Officer, Patient Experience and Engagement Program, UChicago Medicine

I

IF ONLY I GOT A 'DO-OVER'

"I did then what I knew how to do.
Now that I know better, I do better."

— Maya Angelou

Recently, I was driving my parents home from a concert we had attended together. It was late in the evening with very little moonlight, making the road difficult for my mother to see. As my mom sat in the passenger seat, watching me maneuver through the streets, and unable to imagine herself being capable of such a skill, she turned to me and said - "You do everything so perfectly." And, while I know this statement to certainly not be true, right there, in that moment, much of what guided my actions, attitudes and behaviors throughout my career was present - the desire to do my best to achieve perfection in everything I did. Even as I write, I can hear the ridiculousness of this. It's almost embarrassing, as I connect to the egocentric core of this belief.

As an employee, this was my mantra - do your best, please the boss, work diligently to go above and beyond, and be recognized for your work performance. And as a manager, and later a leader in multiple organizations, this same philosophy was the engine behind the drive that fueled my leadership approach and expectations of others - if *they* do *their* best and perform well - really well, they will be recognized and rewarded.

I was the leader who could motivate the 'hard workers' to achieve impossible tasks. I could build incredible teams that accomplished extraordinary feats. And, I never minimized celebrating and recognizing those that performed. I was also the leader who was easily frustrated and dismissive with those individuals who did not share my mantra of perfection and performance.

It Was All About the Work

As a new leader, I was often reminded of the notion to model the behavior, walk the talk, and BE the change... and I practiced this philosophy. But, as I later realized, the root of this idea for me, was that it was all about the work and getting the work done perfectly. I modeled the behaviors of 'hard working', being organized, paying attention to the details, delivering complete reports, showing up on time, leaving late. I walked the talk of an employee committed to excellence, who worked tirelessly to meet (and most often exceed) the expectations of my boss and the organizational objectives. This logic of, "If I do, others should too", guided my leadership practices, expecting each individual to follow my lead, and mirror my commitment and performance aspirations.

Early on, as part of my leadership development, I was 'asked' to attend a nationally recognized leadership development program; a week-long training class focused on team building and motivating others in a positive way. I remember thinking what a good team builder I was, and being curious what I might learn from this developmental experience. As part of the curriculum, we were asked to take the Myers Briggs personality assessment. Nearly forty years later, I remember vividly receiving the results. I was an ESTJ (Extrovert, Sensing, Thinking, Judging). And I reveled in this assignment of personality traits! It described me perfectly.

I was energetic, could solve any problem, I was logical and decisive. I was the person you could count on to get the job done. And, as an employee and a leader, these qualities certainly helped me to advance my career.

While at the leadership center, I also learned, in a very sort of 'aha' moment, that other people did not share my same personality preferences. *(I know what you are thinking - Really?!?)* The idea that not everyone was like me, particularly when it was all about the work, was eye opening. I realized then, that to be an effective leader, I (not they) had to change my approach to motivating, encouraging, and guiding individuals and teams. This was incredibly enlightening. And yet, I still got it all wrong.

I Got it All Wrong

Where I got it totally wrong was that I still thought my role was to guide my staff to perform at a level where someday they would reach my same level of 'perfectionism', excellence and drive. My leadership practices remained centered on the work - the task, the project, and in adopting the consideration of others' personality preferences. believed that my role was to be cognizant of their 'starting point' in needing direction to adopt a work ethic and commitment to excellence that mirrored mine.

Incredible as it sounds, it didn't occur to me that shifting from 'it's all about me' to 'it's all about them' was at the crux of a caring, understanding, and motivating leadership style. It seems so clear today, but back then, because I so very often met and exceeded the organizational objectives and expectation of my leaders, I was blind, and even conflicted to the need to consider EVERY individual as magnificent, creative and capable, and approach my motivational, engagement, and leadership strategies that honored their best qualities. In fact, quite the opposite. My practice of driving individuals to be more like me, many times resulted in actions and behaviors that were not only demotivating and certainly unengaging, but were disrespectful, inconsiderate, unappreciative and mean. *(And yes, it feels really icky to say this in print.)*

Shifting from 'it's all about
me' to 'it's all about them'
was at the crux of a caring,
understanding, and motivating
leadership style.

And worse, I was often consciously aware of these 'bad' behaviors - particularly after the fact, as they were incongruent with what I valued, who I was as a person, and certainly what I wanted to be as a leader. And this profoundly affected me. I was unhappy, I felt defeated, I lost my sense of self and found absolutely no joy in the work that I had so loved doing. There were multiple times that I would drive home from work wishing I could have a 'do-over' - in a meeting, a one-on-one encounter, a conversation. I replayed over and over in my head, how the individual was affected by my words, my tone, and my non-verbal body language. I could hear, in their responses to my probing questions and declarative statements, their defensiveness, their indifference, their detached commitment to the work, the organization and to me.

My Defining Moment

Trying to mirror the behaviors of what I understood to be effective, combined with this incredibly ridiculous drive toward perfection, had blocked my ability to adopt any other leadership approach... until I saw my reflection in the behaviors of an executive leader I reported to. It was, for me, my defining moment. During this time, I was promoted into leadership positions that were new areas of responsibility for me. I was unfamiliar with the subject matter and struggled to find the pathway toward 'perfect', frequently failing to reach my specified goals. I was often defensive when asked to provide status updates. Each conversation felt like I was getting in trouble, with constant interruptions, tones of disappointment and an energy of uninterested indifference. I would find myself horrified at how I was treated as a person, wondering how my boss could not see how hard I was working, trying, performing. It was demoralizing, defeating and dispiriting.

I remember, quite vividly, the day of this defining awakening. I was sitting in my office, getting ready for a conference call to provide an update on a project. I had worked tirelessly to meet the deadline and even solicited the help of others to ensure I would meet the requirements outlined in previous conversations. I was (so I thought) confident, prepared and ready for the update. Not long after I started sharing my update, my boss began, in a very condescending and unimpressed tone, to point out the shortcomings of my efforts. My presentation wasn't succinct enough, I had too many details, I didn't have enough…. I should have this… or shouldn't have that. I could feel my emotions rising and recognized that my responses to the unrelenting critical comments had a clear tone of defensiveness. To make matters worse, I was called out on my attitude and then informed that we would now be having a 'teachable' moment about responses to constructive criticism.

It was at this moment that I realized that how I felt was how my employees might feel when I was offering them 'constructive criticism'. And I didn't like it one bit. Looking in the metaphorical mirror was difficult. It was not an image I was proud of, nor one that I wanted to manifest in my personal way of BEING and certainly not one to bring forward further into my leadership practices.

A New Way of BEING

So, I made a conscious, intentional decision to change - to be kind and to care for every individual that I had the privilege to work with and to lead, and to bring my most authentic best self to every encounter. I made the conscious choice to shift from leading the work to leading people in a way that discovers the best in each individual, leveraging their strengths and holding up the mirror to their magnificence.

> I made the conscious choice
> to shift from leading the work
> to leading people in a way
> that discovers the best in
> each individual.

This new way of BEING has been transformative… for me professionally and personally. Today, I lead less from the head and more from the heart. I am happier. I am joyful. I have meaningfulness and purpose in the work that I do. The people that I connect with, and lead, matter… to me. And quite frankly, I like me and the positive energy I bring into my life and leadership practices. And this, my friends, has created a contagious change among those around me. The excited and enthusiastic energy that I bring into the room is visibly welcomed and immediately sets the tone for any conversation. Smiles, presence and genuine interest are reciprocated, further energizing the encounter with significance and positively reinforcing this new way of BEING. Appreciation, gratitude and respect ripple through the interaction, quietly acknowledging our collective capacity to achieve new levels of organizational potential, while at the same time, making a difference in people's lives.

Leading hArtfully

Leading hArtfully is about the art and the heart (hence, hArt) of leadership. It is an invitation to bring your best self forward further to discover and leverage the best in others. There are skills and frameworks, practices and principles, for sure, to be noted throughout this book. But getting to the art and heart of leading, finding your flow, the eloquence and grace within you, and connecting at the heart level with each individual is an experience not to be missed, as it holds the possibility of a most magnificent journey of leading others. Leading hArtfully is an invitation to not only discover your best leader self, but to experience the realization that, when you choose to discover the best in others, there are powerfully positive shifts in individual well-BEING and fulfillment. And, most importantly, it is an invitation to acknowledge the impact you make in the individual lives of those you lead that together, through your vision and guidance, can achieve new levels of organizational performance and individual engagement.

Leading hArtfully begins with a conscious intention to discover the best in people and to bring forward further this way of BEING into your day to day leadership practices. Mindful shifts in what you choose to notice, what attitudes you choose to hold, what conversations you choose to create, and what actions you choose to take are all components of leading hArtfully. And each of these is grounded in the belief that each individual has within themselves the capacity to be their best.

Leading hArtfully begins with a conscious intention to discover the best in people.

Leading hArtfully, and those things you will discover, practice and (perhaps) adopt from this book, is intended to be an evolutionary journey of discovery. There will be moments of curiosity and certainly moments when you say to yourself - 'of course, that makes sense'. But knowing information does not change behavior or practice. Stepping deeper into the space where curiosity shifts to trial, inviting conscious, intentional, 'on-purpose' awareness, reflection and action leads to transformative change. Understanding what is meaningful to you in your choice to bring your heart and best self into your leader practices, and appreciating what shifts you are seeing as a result of a new action, attitude or behavior, may certainly lead to finding a deeper sense of fulfillment and achievement for you.

Adopting a practice of leading hArtfully, leveraging individual strengths and holding up the mirror to those concrete instances where individual best selves are present are undeniable proven practices, and arguably effective stepping stones to improved performance, outcomes, results, and engagement. And, while those are important elements of organizational leadership, my hope for you as you explore these principles and practices is that you will find and discover how, when leading hArtfully, YOU are BEING your best leader self, and experiencing all of the energy, positive emotions and individual engagement (aka flow) that go with doing and BEING your best leader self!

There is a catalogue of expected skills essential for any leader within the operational and managerial landscape - independent of industry. There are books and blogs, frameworks and fundamentals, training and teaching institutions aimed at equipping leaders to communicate effectively, develop trust, earn respect, engage the workforce, foster diversity, manage change, and achieve business objectiveness. Take a look at any resume and you'll find a host of leadership skills highlighted - goal setting, team building, problem solving, delegating, coaching, resolving conflict, listening, collaborating, innovating, negotiating, analyzing performance and data analysis… to name a few.

> Having the skills alone - knowing the science behind the behaviors - may not be enough to inspire the best from your employees.

And each of these is an essential skill. They are, if you will, the periodic table of the science of leadership; every element is essential to the structure of the leadership construct you are creating. These skills are unquestionably the science behind the chemistry of connecting, relating, inspiring, engaging and leading. However, having the skills alone - knowing the science behind the behaviors - may not be enough to inspire the best from your employees.

- . - . - . - . - . - . - . -

Discovering the best in others requires art. There is an art to leadership - comfortably, confidently and authentically navigating through conversations and interactions that encourage individuals forward, in the direction that you have set, and inspiring each of them to reach new levels of potential and performance in a fulfilling manner. There is also a heart to leadership, caring deeply for the individual, and relating as human beings in an individualized and personalized manner, in the moment, authentically, and listening with the intention to understand the 'who' - not the 'what' - to discover the magnificence that exists within each individual. This art-and-heart is at the core of the leading hArtfully formula.

Listen with the intention to understand the 'who' - not the 'what.'

I have often thought of the science, art and heart of leadership, together, in sync with your way of BEING, fostering relationships, influencing behaviors and cultivating cultures, as something much like a waltz. There is a science to dancing a waltz - the distinctive steps and timing of 1, 2, 3 or step, slide, close, that creates a pattern, uniquely recognizable as a waltz. The science is those basic steps needed to bring the dance forward. Yet, even with those steps, without the artistic flow of movement intertwined with the impassioned heart of the dancer, the waltz is nothing more than a box-step, repeated pattern. It is the art that begins to bring a flow to the dance - where you begin to move gracefully around the room comfortably and confidently, having competently mastered the basic steps. Bits of yourself, your way of BEING, are added into the art - the way you hold your head, the position of your arms, the expression on your face all become a part of the dance and add to the artistic way in which you maneuver around the room, together with your partner.

The next level of experience comes when you bring your heart into the dance. There is an emotional connection to the music and its interpretation through the dance and movements that you create. This connection is felt by those around you as well, the audience palpably experiencing the emotional energy, captivated by the magnificence of the dance.

Much like dancing the waltz, within this book you will study the science of leading hArtfully, taking in the information and frameworks that are presented. Yet, moving forward and adopting a new way of BEING requires courage, choice and commitment to step into a space of discovery, bringing your art and heart forward, evolving and mastering your leadership dance through consistent practice, reflection and action, finding your flow in leading hArtfully.

II
EVERYONE HAS THE CAPACITY TO CHANGE A WORLD

"Never doubt that a small group of thoughtful committed citizens can change the world. Indeed, it is the only thing that ever has."

-Margaret Mead

I have, for as long as I can remember, struggled with what my purpose was in life. Why was I on this planet? I believed that we were all here for something meaningful and defining, yet I couldn't figure out or connect to what that was for me. Having children seemed like a purposeful response to the universe's calling for meaning, but when that was not physiologically feasible, I was left to continue the exploration of meaning. I loved my work, and often found meaning in what I did, but there was still a large void. It wasn't personal. I wasn't connected to a 'humanness' that I seemed to be in constant search of.

My Search for Purpose

My search for purpose was amplified by my desire to consciously shift my leadership focus to discovering the best in each individual. Intellectually, I understood what and how I wanted to be as a leader, but found it difficult to adopt these new-found leadership qualities and BE different. Without an emotional connection to understanding the significance of my intention, I couldn't find my way forward to make this change.

Everything changed one morning in February. I was in New Jersey attending a company team meeting that was hosted at a nearby hotel. It seemed like a typical winter day in the northeast, bitter cold outside, with little sun. The meeting room was located in a secluded area of the hotel on the first floor, although it had the feel of a basement. The walls were painted a dark green, with long hallways and no artwork. The carpet was equally dark and the low ceilings made it feel like a cave. My mood mirrored the environment - low energy, non-engaging attitude and wearing a bland expression. Taking a break from the meeting, I went in search of the vending machines for some chocolate treats.

As I was walking down the hallway, I could see one of the maintenance men approaching me. He blended into the background with his uniform of olive green pants and shirt, making him almost 'invisible'. I noticed as he made his way down the hallway, that his persona also appeared to mirror the environment. His head was down, and his pace slow. As he got closer, I glanced at his name embroidered on his shirt, and almost instinctively I cheerfully, and quite personably, said - "Good Morning, Carl."

He instantly looked up and, with the biggest smile, that brought his eyes to light, he nodded and greeted me back. I immediately felt energized with delight. It was then that everything changed. Immediately, I realized that I had the capacity to change a world. That morning, I changed Carl's world. It was as if I had this superpower to make him un-invisible. I had, in that moment, connected to my purpose in life. For so long, I had been thinking that my purpose was something grand, large, and extraordinary. Never did I imagine that, within the simplicity of a smile, I would discover meaningfulness in my life. So, there it was, my purpose - 'to bring a smile to everyone I encounter'.

> It was as if I had this superpower to make him un-invisible.

That moment also brought further clarity to the persona I wanted to bring to my leadership style. I wanted to BE that person who had the capacity to change a world - through kindness, caring, and BEING my authentic self - with each person I encountered, including my staff and colleagues. This became my new mantra and led the way forward toward discovering the best in people.

Accessing Your Superpower

I really liked the idea of changing A world. It seemed that my own capacity to change a world of a person, a moment, a situation, was doable. I realized that I do have the capacity to change a world - to create a positive energy that brings about an amazing change. And, empowered with my choice to change a world, and the awareness of the effect when leaning more fully and consciously into that choice, I felt I had narrowed my search for purpose.

Changing A world is also relatable to others. When I hear stories of 'change-a-world' moments created by colleagues, it's not the lifesaving moments that are shared, or the grand gestures taken for the world to see, but rather, change-a-world moments are those simple, kind, meaningful, personal acts of self, where we give our heart to each other, that help to make a difference in someone's life.

Change-a-world moments are also tangible. Many times, I could see the immediate impact of my actions in changing a world. And this became important in reinforcing this new way of BEING, creating a new pattern of behavior or habit. I often would make a practice of going to busy coffee shops and watch quietly as the cashiers and baristas would attend to the many customers. I noticed their intent focus on getting the orders quickly and accurately, repeating back to the customer the order description and taking payments; only to move to the next person in quickfire fashion. It seemed so impersonal - on both sides of the counter. Neither individual acknowledged the person with whom they were connecting. Their interactions were all about the work and reminiscent of my earlier focus as a leader.

Bringing my practice of changing a world to the cafes was simple. In the throes of the busyness of taking orders and making coffee drinks, I would approach the counter, ready to place my order. And, as the cashier quickly asked what I wanted, I would access my superpower to make people *un-invisible*, read their name from their apron and offer a huge smile and a greeting, slowing the pace of the café and shifting the energy and focus. "Hello Mary", I would say. "How is your day going?" Sometimes I would offer an acknowledgement of something uniquely magnificent about their presence, or how they quickly and cheerfully could take an order. My energy was always intentional - positive and certainly enthusiastic, which made for a reciprocal, contagious response. Most often, I would receive a brilliant smile back, with an almost unsaid 'thank you for seeing me' nod. And, again there it was, another change-a-world moment... and I created it.

Change-A-World Moments...At Work

The awareness I had, of not only having the capacity to create these moments, but experiencing the associated joy and positive emotion, was profound, and fueled my desire to create more. I began, also, to notice how other people created change-a-world moments. And if I turned my observations to look for these, I could see them everywhere… simple gestures of kindness, small gifts of generosity, innocuous conversations - all of which helped another person to feel that they mattered. As I centered my attention on these observations, I was curious if others experienced joy, happiness and fulfillment when they were connected to a purpose or something meaningful in their life.

I brought this curiosity to work one evening. I was scheduled to do an observational coaching session with an emergency medicine physician - Dr. Dan. It was a Friday night at a high patient volume urban hospital. The waiting room was filled with patients wanting to be seen 'now', with little tolerance, understanding and patience for the challenges the nurses and physicians faced in trying to see and treat the many individuals in need of help. The main area of the Emergency Department (ED) was full - sicker patients in beds waiting to be admitted, with nurses and doctors doing their best to manage the clinical and workflow challenges a Friday night emergency room brings. The energy and tone of the conversations were filled with frustration, negativity and exhaustion, a common condition in the ED environment.

> I could see them everywhere… simple gestures of kindness, small gifts of generosity, innocuous conversations - all of which helped another person to feel that they mattered.

Wanting to put into practice this notion of discovering change-a-world moments, I created an intention to shift my observations and focus from the operational challenges and process inefficiencies, universally present throughout the ED, to consciously 'turning my (new) observer on' and calibrated it to notice how these extraordinary emergency medicine individuals were using their superpowers to let patients (and colleagues) know that they mattered and that they were *un-invisible* to them. As you might expect, this was no easy task, as the ED was filled with chaos and high intensity drama. Those simple, soft and quiet meaningful actions are easily hidden amongst the literal and figurative noise of such an environment.

The first opportunity I had to turn my observer on was in following an ED technician out to the waiting room. She was tasked with bringing an elderly man from the waiting room back to the treatment area. Now, before I describe what happened, it is important to understand a little bit about ED technicians (aka Techs) and their role in the ED. You see, ED Techs are the kings and queens of multitasking. They are responsible for moving patients, readying rooms, starting IVs, performing EKGs, replenishing supplies, and assisting in clinical procedures, to name just a few of their responsibilities. They rarely sit still, shifting quickly from one task to the next, anticipating their next assignment, and moving rapidly to get it done. Taking time to create a meaningful connection with a patient was something I didn't expect to see - particularly with a non-calibrated observer.

The ED Tech approached the elderly man in the waiting room. He was in his mid-70s, tall and quite thin. He was seated in a wheelchair, making it easy to transport him to the back. She introduced herself. This was an easy exchange, with no interaction on his part. She then began to wheel him back. As she was maneuvering past the other patients, the elderly man began to vomit into the plastic tub in his lap. What happened next caught my attention. With my observer turned on, and calibrated to notice change-a-world moments, I saw how she immediately stopped the wheel chair and bent down to gently rub his back. With her eyes focused on his tired face, she comforted him with her words. In a gentle tone, she let him know that he would be taken care of, and that his team of doctors and nurses were waiting to help him feel better.

With my observer still calibrated, I watched how he responded. It was evident in his eyes and with a quiet nod that he also 'saw' her, and understood that she 'saw' him. In that moment, both of those individuals had made each other *un-invisible*, and brought meaningfulness and purpose to their individual actions. I was moved by this event, nearly bringing tears to my eyes. Something as simple as a pause amongst the commotion of the situation, coupled with a personalized connection, had created a profound moment of caring. I had just witnessed a change-a-world moment!

After a while, I approached the ED Tech and shared my observation with her. I wanted to acknowledge her for these most profound actions and the positive, resultant consequence. As I shared the details of what I noticed, uncovering her gentleness in how she stopped the wheel chair to comfort the gentleman, and offering reassurance with her words, I could see that it was difficult for her to connect to the meaningfulness and the profound impact of her actions and way of BEING. She humbly replied saying, "It's what I do. It's my job." Trying to convince her to notice her actions as something beyond the routine of her work responsibilities was futile. The tasks she was charged with carrying out, twelve hours each day, in a fast paced, time-sensitive, productivity prioritized environment, had overcome her ability to see her capacity to change a world. Not only did she not see this capacity, I further realized that neither her colleagues, leaders nor administration chose to observe, reinforce and cultivate a culture that acknowledges these most magnificent moments.

As the night continued, I spent the rest of my time in the ED, seeing patients with Dr. Dan. My observations expanded to see beyond effective communication skills and into a new level of impact and intention. My coaching conversations with Dan shifted from what he did, to what he noticed in how he connected with his patients. My questions to him prompted reflections and context that helped him to (re)connect to why he went into healthcare. I invited him to 'turn his observer on' and to calibrate it to notice his capacity and choice to change a world. We spent the evening together with his patients, holding up the mirror to the personal impact he made with each patient, in a way that extended beyond the superb clinical care he provided, and into the heart of the interaction.

Here's a glimpse into Dr. Dan's experience:

The patients Dr. Dan saw that evening ranged from a teenage stabbing victim who required Dan to insert a tube into his chest to save his life, to a rancher who, in an attempt to corral his cattle, got his thumb caught in a rope, ripping it off his hand. Watching the clinical team calmly and ever so efficiently bring these life-and-limb-saving actions forward was something I will forever recall as a significantly profound experience. Those lifesaving moments were clearly impactful to the patients, forever changed as a result of Dan's efforts.

But none were as meaningful (to me and Dan) as the woman who was in the emergency department that evening for the chronic back pain she was experiencing, yet again. She was a patient who had been to the ED on multiple prior occasions in search of explanations, comfort and answers. Walking into her room, it was immediately evident that she was frustrated with not having a cause or cure, and ever so tired of the debilitating pain she was experiencing

Dan began his conversation with an assessment of her clinical presentation and uncovering the relevant and important elements of her medical history, confidently and competently. He skillfully and masterfully maneuvered through the work of a physician, evaluating, diagnosing and treating.

Yet, his clinical expertise wasn't what stood out that evening amongst the major interventions he would bring to his emergency room critical patients. It was his way of BEING - his capacity to offer empathy and understanding to this woman who desperately wanted relief. It was his capacity to listen and connect to this patient, in such a way that she felt heard and her truth of her experience validated. Sitting next to her, he offered no judgements or comments relative to her story, but met her where she was at, taking the time and opening up the space for her to share comfortably. His smile was always present, and his tone of voice calming.

It was also the way in which Dan created a conversation with her that stood out; putting her (metaphorically) in the center of the dialogue with his questions and observations, asking for her input and acknowledging her responses. He was kind and patient. Dancing in the moment with her. His mannerisms personified those of a person who cared deeply for another human being. He had stepped beyond the head-centric scientific work of a physician and stepped into a personalized, heart-centric space of caring for others - offering hope and healing, leveraging his choice and capacity to change a world.

At the close of the shift that evening, I offered my observations and together we explored, through a coaching conversation, his own discoveries and meaningful reflections. Our conversation prompted a very profound experience that shaped the way he practices medicine, even today. Holding up the mirror for him to see his magnificence, and reconnecting his work to purpose and meaningfulness (to him) prompted this enlightened reflection.

"... And holding that lady's hand, and 'being in the moment' with her reminds me that it may not be that big of a deal for me, but maybe it was for her... And when she started crying because at least we have something to try and fix, I felt really proud to have offered her a little hope. I thought to myself, it's really not about the disease, it's about the people and how the work we do affects them, not their pathology... I have had a few very profound experiences that have shaped the way I practice and how I "see myself in this world"... (this) reminded me of how lucky and blessed I am to have the chance to do the work I do."

The Role of Leadership in Creating Change-A-World Moments

In turning my observer on and bringing awareness to individuals of their capacity to change a world, I too, was changing a world.

This notion of bringing visibility to and (re)connecting purpose and meaningfulness to my healthcare colleagues became the focus of my work - assisting individuals, leaders and organizations to discover the best in each other and to cultivate cultures that, first and foremost, acknowledge and value each individual, and secondly, the work they do. It was also what (re)connected me to a way of BEING that facilitated a profound shift in my leadership style. I realized that, in turning my observer on and bringing awareness to individuals of their capacity to change a world, I too, was changing a world.

Bringing this practice of noticing and acknowledging change-a-world moments is purposeful and intentional. It requires a fundamental shift in what I choose to believe about those I work with, and requires a conscious action in what I choose to observe and in how I offer acknowledgements. As leaders (and as individuals), we have a choice in how we show up each day to influence the work environment and the individuals within that environment.

Leading hArtfully is an invitation into a new way of leadership BEING, a new way to show up, if you will. It offers joy, purpose, meaningfulness and potential (individual and organizational).

And it begins with turning your observer on.

III
TURNING YOUR OBSERVER ON

One of the things that stood out in my coach training was the notion that change - a shift from the current state to the desired state - occurs when there is meaningfulness attached to that shift. In other words, change occurs when we are connected to what is important to us about that change. Whether it is a change in lifestyle, a change in jobs, a change in behavior, a change in... change is productive and effective when there is something individually important connected to it. In short, individual change occurs when it is important to the individual.

Turning your observer on, consciously and intentionally focusing your observations and attention to discovering the best in people, is quite frankly, a change. And for many leaders, it could be a potentially big change. So, finding what is meaningful (to you) in turning your observer on will become vitally important and critically essential.

Taking Care of Strangers

Thinking back on that Friday night in the ED… while I was certainly prepared, intellectually, to look for and observe what Dr. Dan was 'doing right' in his patient interactions, I wasn't prepared to witness the depth of kindness and caring that occurred between patients and caregivers. Not having a clinical background, and absent of any direct responsibility within the ED environment, helped me, I am convinced, to witness the many impactful moments of humanity created by the ED professionals. And certainly, not having any responsibility to take care of patients offered me the ability to simply sit and observe. Sitting at the nurses' station in the middle of the ED, I watched each individual move in sync to the dance of the evening, orchestrated by the many clinical presentations that were continuously arriving, and thinking to myself how incredibly profound it was that these clinical experts - nurses, physicians, physician assistants, technicians, radiologists - were taking care of strangers.

This notion of taking care of strangers was difficult for me to comprehend. I couldn't personally connect to caring at that level for another person that I didn't know, that wasn't related to me, or someone that I didn't know anything about. I began to question the degree to which I could unselfishly choose to help another individual, making my observations of their individualized way of calming and connecting that much more impactful.

> How incredibly profound it was that these clinical experts were taking care of strangers.

Within this 'mini' conversation I was having with myself, I could hear the presence of the judgments I was making of others and of myself. It was almost as if I had been limiting the reality that, within the walls of this ED, existed the best in humanity and, certainly, the best in healthcare. What was predominant within this new awareness was that my (old) observer was calibrated from past experiences, interactions and observations… experiences that I had rated as 'less than' caring. In fact, what I realized was that I was choosing to notice (first) what was 'wrong' with how we cared for individuals versus what was 'right' in the meaningful and magnificent care we (clinical and non-clinical healthcare professionals) deliver to those in need. This was keenly instrumental in my choice to create an intention to (re)calibrate my observer and shift my observations and leadership way of BEING to discover the best in people.

Calibrating Your Observer

The timing of this awareness and choice to discover the best in others coincided with my coach training and reinforced the value of this shift in mindset and perspective. Fundamental to a person-centered coaching practice is the ability to uncover and highlight individual strengths within our clients (aka - their best self) to leverage forward in making a change in performance, learning and/or fulfillment. This approach, known as strengths-based, to motivating change was new to me and certainly required a deliberate, conscious, thoughtful intention. Having graduated from college with a math degree, and later specialized in quality and performance improvement, my brain and behaviors were wired to fix things. I was equipped and skilled in identifying problems and analyzing root causes to implement appropriate, effective, and permanent corrective action. It was foreign, unfamiliar and even a bit unbelievable to look for and leverage strengths as a means toward improvement.

Committed to this journey (and also wanting to pass the coaching certification exam), I set out to calibrate my observer to discover the strengths or 'best self' qualities and characteristics in my colleagues, my staff and coaching clients.

This was not easy. And went way beyond trying to 'catch' someone doing something 'right'. In fact, what I discovered is that it had little to do with the individual I was observing, and everything to do with me. I recognized that I had to take a step back and fundamentally believe that, within each individual, there is the capacity to do and BE their best. Calibrating my observer required me to set aside any judgments and/ or preconceived assumptions I had about them and their abilities, and step into a space of believing in their best selves. Most difficult, and most important, was the need to also set aside my own ego and be open to not being the 'expert', in an endeavor to see them as their authentic best self, capable of, and choosing to, make a difference in the world. Accessing my super-power to see strengths, characteristics and qualities, I would soon learn, required intention and practice. Lots of practice!

> I had to take a step back and fundamentally believe that, within each individual, there is the capacity to do and BE their best.

The Default Observer

Nearly ten years into my practice of turning my observer on to discover the best in others, I still find my observer sometimes stuck in the (previous) default position of looking for what's 'wrong'. This was never so evident as one evening when I was observing Neil, an emergency medicine nurse working the night shift. My session began at 7:30pm and was planned to finish around 10:30pm.

Truth be told, the night shift observation sessions are not my preference, as I really do 'enjoy' my sleep. Nevertheless, there I was, standing on the outskirts of their department huddle, listening to the evening announcements and challenges being shared amongst the ED team of clinical experts. Scanning the sea of navy blue scrubs, I found Neil, a relatively new nurse from the Philippines.

I had met Neil before. He had attended one of my workshops, and in saying "Hello" to him, I quickly recalled his quiet demeanor and the difficulty I often had in understanding what he was saying through his Philippines accent. And, there it was, almost immediately present, the default observer, already judging and anticipating countless patient interactions where the patient would not understand a word he shared.

Neil, like most clinical healthcare professionals I have had the privilege of observing, was a fast walker, moving through the ED at a pace that definitely required flat shoes - not a typical fashion accoutrement found in my wardrobe. As the before-shift huddle of staff adjourned, Neil quickly moved to meet with the dayshift nurse assigned to the patients he would now be responsible to care for. As I stood there, listening to the two of them discuss the clinical needs of the patient, I couldn't help but hear that he was assigned to four patients (versus three), another operational issue my default observer had honed in on.

Realizing, through my own self-awareness, the challenge I was having in looking past the operational and individual 'opportunities' the ED environment was presenting to me, I made a concerted, intentional effort to shift my mindset and observations to Neil and the purpose of my visit - to hold up the mirror to how he would create positive, impactful, caring, therapeutic relationships with his patients.

Again, mindfully armed with my conscious intention to discover the best in others, and with my observer now appropriately calibrated, I immediately noticed Neil's palpable positive energy, and how it came to life the minute he set foot into the emergency department. And, with a smile that would brighten anyone's day, Neil began his shift saying "Hello" to each one of his co-workers he encountered. His greeting was purposeful in making a connection and welcomed by each colleague, as evidenced by their returned smile and personalized "Hello." I specifically recall one occasion, as he was rushing through the ED to respond to a patient's needs, when he came upon a new employee. He stopped, introduced himself and welcomed the new nurse, reassuring him that he was not alone. In the back of my mind, I was noting that he was creating multiple 'mini' change-a-world moments, accessing his superpower to make each individual un-invisible and letting them know they mattered… to him.

Neil's purposeful connection was not limited to colleagues. He consistently personalized his interactions with patients, anticipating their needs and reassuring them that he would be taking good care of them. One interaction, in particular, really stood out that evening. It was a cancer patient who had arrived earlier with incredible pain, was terribly uncomfortable, and looked immensely distressed. And, although he wasn't able to give her any additional pain medications, he was able to make her feel comfortable and cared for. I remember vividly how he acknowledged and responded to her pain, bringing her a cold cloth for relief, and consistently updating her on the availability of an inpatient bed – each and every time he walked into the room – which was VERY often. And, in response to his actions, her words, body language, and expressions indicated her appreciation and awareness that he was taking care of her!

You Might Be Surprised

That night, there was never a more vivid example of empathy, humanity and world-changing moments than how Neil chose to show up to care for his patients. Nevertheless, it required a conscious intentional action to turn my observer on to discover the best in Neil. Watching him care for each of his patients to create genuine, meaningful human connections was not only enlightening and inspiring, but validated the need to continue to change the conversation from what's 'wrong' to what's 'right'. Constant reinforcement of the 'need for improvement', without a balance of acknowledging the magnificence that each individual brings into their care of others contributes to feeling unappreciated, lack of confidence, exhaustion (emotional and physical) and lack of joy, and certainly not congruent with a leadership way of BEING I wanted to embody.

Holding up the mirror to an individual's best self is an important element of leadership that can help to engage staff in what is meaningful, productive and positive to them; contributing to cultivating a culture where caring, therapeutic relationships occur. Quieting the default observer and shifting your observations and responses to discover the best can be challenging, especially when we have advanced up the leadership career ladder looking for what to fix and demonstrating our competence to improve business performance. We are skilled and trained to identify problems and implement solutions. We are practiced at giving feedback to improve performance. And, we are comfortable stepping in to outline, orchestrate and oversee improved outcomes.

> Holding up the mirror
> to an individual's best self
> is an important element
> of leadership.

And while these practices are important to continue, I am suggesting that a shift in mindset, observations and acknowledgement that leverage the best in each individual can offer similar results and, perhaps, even more. Noticing and acknowledging their actions, attitudes and behaviors (what they do) that support a mission of caring for others, together with the individual unique strengths, characteristics and qualities (who they are BEING) they hold within themselves and share with others, positively reinforces those behaviors and qualities that you not only want to see more of, but drive performance excellence. Kick-starting this practice of strengthening and encouraging their best selves begins with turning your observer on and pretending that it is connected to a flashlight. And, when you see individuals Doing and BEING their best, shining the light on them, bringing your observations to their awareness. Turning your observer on and acknowledging their best selves fosters trust and deepens the relationship, essential ingredients to new levels of performance, potential and possibility.

Leading hArtfully is an invitation to step forward further into your most authentic leader self, turning your observer on to discover the best in others, and changing the conversation from what's 'wrong' to what's 'right'.

And, in doing so, just like my night with Neil, you might just be surprised what you discover.

IV
A NEW PATHWAY

Discovering the Best in People

There is a host of research and literature that supports a strengths-based, appreciative approach to foster increased levels of performance, engagement and well-BEING. Experts in psychology, neuroscience, human resources and leadership have written books, research papers, articles and blogs that are easily accessible to bring credibility and understanding to your strengths-based leadership practice.

Of course, the first question to be addressed in adopting a new practice is - Why? - Why a strengths-based, appreciative approach? The short answer is, when you discover the best in people, they feel their best. And, when they feel their best, they do their best work. Discovering the best in others - noticing and acknowledging their strengths and accomplishments helps them to feel more confident. It enhances their well-BEING, as they are experiencing elements of positive emotion, fulfillment and accomplishment. They feel appreciated and valued, which I imagine if I were to ask any one of you, is what you want for your staff. Let's not forget engaged... individually engaged in the work they do, recognizing the impact and contribution they make, and feeling connected to the organization is strategically imperative to business performance.

> When you discover the best in people, they feel their best. And, when they feel their best, they do their best work.

But simply knowing what the literature says and why it might be important to bring a strengths-based approach into your leadership way of BEING, does not change behavior. Exploring and bringing clarity to what is meaningful to you in wanting to adopt a new pathway forward is essential for making this leadership shift. Answering 'why consider changing?' is essential. After all, your current way of leading has been effective. It is, in part, how you have matured and demonstrated your leadership capabilities that resulted in your promotion to the position that you hold today. The old pathway of leadership is also what you are comfortable with. That 'shoe fits'. So, what is your 'why' behind wanting to bring new elements of leading hArtfully - artfully leading through your heart - to your interactions and approach?

Let's pause for a moment and jump into a simulated semi-coaching conversation… with just a few questions that might prompt this exploration.

- - · - · - · - · - ·

- *What is important about leading hArtfully to you?*
- *What does this notion of discovering the best in people look like in practice?*
- *What will you notice in your staff when you are leading hArtfully?*
- *How are they interacting with each other?*

- *How might, how you show up (leading hArtfully) influence how they show up?*

- *How will you leave each day, having discovered the best in staff and colleagues?*

- *What best-leader-self qualities and strengths would you continue to bring forward further into leading hArtfully?*

- *As a leader, what might you experience if you were leading from your heart?*

- *What would you notice in yourself?*

- *What image of yourself comes to mind (bring details and clarity to this)?*

- *What would be possible?*

- *How might this impact your department's performance and potential?*

- *And, at the end of the day, filled with acknowledgments of your staff's individual best selves - those actions, attitudes, strengths and qualities - that manifested in meeting the day's operational objectives, what would you acknowledge yourself for?*

Your responses to the questions above can help to jumpstart you forward onto this new pathway. They are conversation starters to guide you to the starting gate of leading hArtfully. Stepping further forward, with a conscious, intentional, and mindful practice initiates the shift from our current state to our desired state. The questions are designed to prompt discovery and bring clarity and specificity to aid in defining your desired state. They help to bring meaningfulness and motivation to why you want to step into a new way of BEING.

conscious and intentional   *coupled with*   *is where*

ACTION + (DISCOVERY & REFLECTION) = CHANGE

occurs

Action - conscious and intentional action, coupled with discovery and reflection - is where change occurs. Taking action promotes a new practice of DOING and BEING, and discovery and reflection bring about 'on-purpose' awareness, inviting a deeper, curious interpretation of the experience with a (potentially) new perspective into possibility and meaning. It is this 'on-purpose' awareness that energizes you with the possibility of a new way of BEING. In other words, it's noticing and acknowledging the impact of what happens, having adopted a new leadership practice that motivates you to continue to move forward further... consciously, intentionally, mindfully.

Justin is a director-level leader within a large organization. Just thinking about him brings a smile, filled with positive energy, to my thoughts. He stands out as a leader who not only cares about the individuals that report to him, but also as someone who wants the best for each individual. He is kind, thoughtful, and reflective, consciously taking in experiences and bringing to his awareness the meaningfulness and impact of his actions. He shows up enthusiastic each day, drawing his colleagues and co-workers into a space of possibility. His staff meetings and huddles are filled with laughter and a comfortableness that invites conversation and stories filled with prideful examples of how his team makes a difference in the lives of those they serve.

'On-purpose' awareness energizes you with the possibility of a new way of BEING.

This notion of 'discovering the best in people' and altering your default observations and predetermined judgements to see the best in each individual, was introduced to Justin as part of a Leading hArtfully leadership workshop. Almost immediately, he remarked that, for him, 'discovering the best' was all about perspective... choosing to consider a new perspective, being open to others' perspectives, and willing to move away from ingrained assumptions, practices and perspectives that previously guided his leadership way of BEING.

He jumped willingly into this practice of discovering the best - consciously and intentionally - choosing what to notice (and to not notice), setting aside judgements and offering each individual a clean slate. He moved quickly to adopt the practice of acknowledging individual strengths, characteristics and qualities, and holding up the mirror to the positive impact each of his staff made each day in the work they did. He was energized by his own actions, attitudes and behaviors, noting the differences he was experiencing in this new leadership approach.

For some time, he continued to bring his best leadership self forward, and after a while, chose to step boldly further into this space of discovering the best. Trusting that his staff had within them the creativity and resourcefulness to do and BE their best, he invited them to participate in the design of an improvement initiative. He consciously shifted his perspective that, as the leader he held all of the answers. He shifted his perspective and belief in the leader as authoritarian to leader as coach. He trusted himself to guide and lead his staff in a way that validated, invited and acknowledged the best in each of them. At the end of his improvement design session he shared:

"It is so exciting to hear the buzz as folks left the room and headed back to their desks. The feedback had been so positive... Allowing them to help direct the workgroups ended up being far more powerful than anything that we could have come up with on our own."

During the session, his employees spoke about what was meaningful to them in the work they did each day, yet again offering a shift in his perspective. He heard that it was important to them to be helpful. He heard again and again that they truly cared about their patients and being able to help them get appointments scheduled, connecting the dots and further appreciating the key role they played in the patients' healing and health. He heard how personal and important the relationships they created with their patients were to each of them. And he realized that the assumptions he was making, thinking they believed the work they did was 'just a job', were utterly misguided in his understanding of why they were a part of his team and now shifted his perspective on why they showed up to work each day.

This experience of attuning to their individual best selves was quite powerful. And, in reflecting on this new-found perspective and leadership way of BEING, he again shared what he discovered:

> *"I heard 'helpfulness' that so many had committed to. I heard their passion in caring for others. I heard the compassion they shared. I heard humanity. It was incredible. I appreciated the evolution they were making from 'that's not my job' to 'let me help!'*

Justin's shift in perspective, and choice to embark on a new pathway of leadership catapulted him into an energy of fulfillment, confidence, and joy. He was energized with the possibility of a new way - fostered through conscious, intentional action and 'on-purpose' awareness. The possibilities realized in this new way of leading were further validated in his performance metrics, exceeding his monthly targets. He was discovering the best in others and in doing so, discovered the best in himself, leveraging both forward and bringing the best to the organization.

Magnificence

Magnifi-cence

*The quality of magnifying the essence or intrinsic nature
(that which is within) of an individual or experience*

Magnificent - I love this word! It has the ability to capture an individual's attention to see the best within themselves. Quite frankly, this is a relatively new word that I've added to my vocabulary, sparked by the observations and awareness I experienced working with and leading healthcare professionals. In fact, this introduction to magnificence came to me one day as I was walking between buildings at a large medical center complex. Meandering through the hallways and lobby were patients and family members of all ages. I saw small children wheeled in strollers by their parent(s), with their brothers and sisters in tow, holding hands together as they traveled together toward their medical appointments. Older individuals were locked arm-in-arm with loved ones, relying on their guidance to help them through this maze of steps needed to support their well-being and health. And, individuals alone, some walking confidently to their destination, others appearing a bit lost (metaphorically and literally), finding their way to the people and places that would help them to feel and be better. The energy of the environment seemed ever so somber and purposeful - they were all there to find help. They were there to find hope.

It was in that moment I saw and experienced the magnificence that existed within each of the many healthcare professionals who dedicate their days and lives to caring for another human being. Immediately, I thought to myself: Where would all of these people go if it were not for the incredible, magnificent individuals at that medical center who devote their time, attention and understanding to those in need? It was equally evident that the magnificence present extended way beyond the nurses and doctors, but with each and every individual the patient encountered along their journey of hope.

As I allowed myself to explore this idea of magnificence further and deeper into my thinking, I wondered: what was the essence of their magnificence? And, in a bold flash of clarity, it was ever so apparent. These individuals, armed with the passion of this most noble profession to care for others, are unselfish. Their actions and intentions are centered and purposefully carried out on behalf of another human being. They are courageous. They are patient and kind. They are incredible problem solvers. They are the kings and queens of multi-tasking. Their attention to detail is impeccable. They have the keen ability to connect with all sorts of individuals, listening and communicating in a way that is respectful and creates collaborative partnerships. They are trustworthy. And they have a reassuring manner that will have lifelong impact. They inspire hope and change worlds.

Yet, even as I write this profound, enlightened reflection, I can almost feel the tug of the old, default leadership mindset pulling toward the other side of this perspective - that yes, they are all that, but... And, time and again, I hear the same opposing viewpoint echoed from leaders when I introduce this concept of magnificence within everyone.

And so I invite you, as a hArtful leader, to consider: what might be possible - in your relationships, levels of engagement, in your individual well-BEING if you were to consistently magnify the essence - the intrinsic nature - of each individual to encourage their best selves?

The Big Aha(!) - A Matter of Significance

Exploring this invitation a bit further, let's begin with the word, 'magnificent', itself. What immediately stands out to me is the suggestion to magnify - m.a.g.n.i.f.i

- to intensify or increase the significance of something. Digging deeper into this model of magnificence, I looked up the definition in the dictionary, and quite frankly realized it didn't capture completely what I was witnessing and appreciating to be magnificent.

So, I made up my own definition - *The quality of magnifying the essence or intrinsic nature (that which is within) of an individual or experience.* It seems that this descriptive meaning not only captures this idea of magnifying - taking action to bring out and enlarge the significance of a characteristic or quality, but also brings into consideration the essence - the intrinsic, genuine nature of the individual; as if to magnify the *significance* of the individual, bringing meaning and purpose to how they matter in this world. And if we are, as leaders, committed to bringing out the best in each individual, then shifting our perspective to see the significance in their individual way of BEING and appreciating their magnificence is essential.

> **Magnify the significance of each individual, bringing meaning and purpose to how they matter in this world.**

Bob is an emergency medicine physician. Clinically, he is one of the finest. He is also one of those doctors who consistently receives multiple accolades from patients and colleagues for having a superb 'bedside manner'. His praises, albeit accurate, were no surprise as I was familiar with the continuous focus and attention he paid to the research, literature, tips and tools in how best to communicate and connect with patients. As the quality leader of his medical group practice, I would often talk with Bob about the 'patient experience', and how best to equip physicians to create exceptional experiences grounded in respect, information sharing and collaboration. What I found ever so interesting in our many conversations, however, was that, even as equipped and expert as he was in knowing 'what to do', he rarely connected the impact he made in BEING his most magnificent self, to the patients' experience of care. In other words, he was blind to the most powerful gift he held in caring for those he served - his intrinsic self. In one of our many conversations around this topic, and with an almost passionate plea to hold up the mirror for him to see his magnificence, he agreed to allow me to observe his patient interactions and to share my observations with him.

I remember our first patient visit vividly. He was seeing an elderly woman who was in the emergency room for chest pain. She had had recurring episodes of shortness of breath, and in response to her children's nudging, had presented to the emergency department to make sure she wasn't having a heart attack. She had little desire to spend any time in the hospital, and certainly was not open to being admitted for observation. As it turned out, there was reason for concern. Of course, Bob explained in detail all of the clinical reasons for his recommendation for admission to the hospital, to which she was more than reluctant. Intuitively, calmly and confidently, he asked her questions to uncover and understand her concerns about staying overnight in the hospital. Bob listened. He listened with the intention to hear the emotional message she was communicating. And he responded. He empathized and, through his tone of voice and kind words, validated her worries and patiently worked together with her to come to a shared agreement around her plan of care. Bob always had a way of comforting the patient and this patient interaction was no different. At the end of the conversation, she agreed to be admitted to the hospital.

As I stood in the corner of the room, I could see how he was connecting with her. I could certainly identify each of the communication techniques and skills that he had studied and brought, ever so meticulously, into the interaction. I had witnessed and experienced his unique qualities of kindness, compassion, and caring that were ever so naturally and authentically present in the way he connected with this patient. It was moving. Again, I was in awe of his personal choice to get up each day, armed with the passion of this most noble of professions, to care for 'strangers'. His magnificence was unmistakable and boldly recognizable. And it was ever so curious to me how he didn't see it.

With Bob in the room, I asked the patient about her visit and interaction with Bob. With a strong tendency toward quality and data, Bob had previously agreed to the 'scale of evaluation' and so, I solicited her rating - good, fair, or I wouldn't bring my dog here. She looked at me and ever decidedly said, "Well, I wouldn't give him a good rating." As you might imagine, this took me, and Bob, completely by surprise. And then she continued. "I would give him an excellent rating." With her radiating smile, and a tone of voice ever so indicative of truth and from the heart, she added - "Because he cares. He cares about me."

"People don't care how much you know until they know how much you care."

In that moment, I glanced at Bob, and I could see his struggle to regulate his emotion. Her response facilitated a glimpse into his magnificence. It was a powerful moment for both Bob and myself. We walked out of the room quietly together. As he walked away to see his next patient, he looked back at me, and I smiled. He understood.

One of Bob's favorite quotes is from Teddy Roosevelt - *"People don't care how much you know until they know how much you care."* That day, Bob understood the true meaning of that quote, and in magnifying the essence of how he connected and cared for his patients, he saw his magnificence.

And then there is Anna. She is a nurse on an in-patient floor in a large metropolitan hospital. I met Anna one day while visiting and connecting with patients on the unit. I was standing in the hallway, when Anna came out of a patient's room. I immediately noticed her smile, beaming from ear to ear. She was documenting something in the patient's medical record when I approached her and said - "Goodness, that smile of yours is the size of Albuquerque!" She smiled, even bigger, back at me, acknowledging my observation.

Wanting to strike up a conversation, I asked her how long she had been working in healthcare and what brought her joy. As you may or may not expect, she responded with - "I love my patients." To which I replied - "Tell me about one of your favorite patients."

The 'Favorite Patient' invitation is what I call a Conversation Starter - and is an effective way to create a conversation that uncovers the magnificence within individuals.

Without pausing, she told me the story of a man who had been in the hospital for more than two weeks. Each day, she would enter his room, bringing her brilliant smile through the door and connecting with him on a personal level. She told me about his family, and what he enjoyed in life. And, as I listened, the essence of her most magnificent self, grew more and more apparent. She was, in a word, lovely. She had an energy that was warm and comforting. She told me how, each day, she listened to his stories and expressed the joy she experienced in getting to know him. She shared how she felt her conversations helped to bring a bit of 'normalcy' to his stay. She loved that she could make him laugh. It was evident that she willingly took the time to BE with him, and used her superpower to make him *un-invisible*. Over the weeks of his stay, they developed a meaningful relationship, and I dare say, she was a bright spot (perhaps the only one) in his day.

As she spoke, I was listening with the intention to acknowledge her, and to bring to light the positive impact she had in the patient's experience of care. As I shared what I heard within her story, magnifying the essence of her best self, I could see her smile grow even larger. She was taking in my words, savoring the recognition, and understanding how she makes a difference in the lives of many. It was her magnificent way of BEING, coupled with the very important clinical work she did that day, and the days that followed, that underscored the significance of how she mattered... to her patients, to me and to herself. And, perhaps, in the words of Buzz Lightyear (from *Toy Story*) 'to infinity and beyond'!

V
HOW YOU SHOW UP MATTERS

Walk the talk, Model the behavior, and Be the change - I really thought I not only understood these leader practices, but that I exemplified them impeccably. I was walking the talk of working hard, modeling the behaviors of going above and beyond and being the example of a conscientious reliable worker. It never occurred to me to show up each day with the intention to bring my best individual self forward (e.g., kind, helpful, caring)… in an endeavor to walk, model, BE and influence how others showed up. Don't get me wrong: I am kind, I am helpful, and I try to be my best self each day. But when I create an intention - a conscious, thoughtful, meaningful intention - a shift occurs in how I show up, manifested through my actions, attitudes and behaviors.

Intentional BEING through Being Intentional

This notion of intentionality and its influence in how I consistently choose to show up became clear one Saturday as I was running in a half marathon. It wasn't my first half marathon. In fact, I'd made a practice of running 6 or 7 half marathons that year. And despite that practice, and the endless training required to achieve a distance of 13.1 miles, I hate running. It is physically challenging, painful and emotionally charged. I am filled with anxiety, and my brain is plagued by the ubiquitous negative thoughts that reinforce the absurd belief that I do not have the ability to successfully finish, to the point that I spend a good part of the first six miles convincing myself not to 'turn around'. I know. Ridiculous!

However, on this particular run it was different. I was blessed with the words of one high school football player as I ran through the 4-mile water station that changed my attitude and the race.

A little background.

As I mentioned earlier, I believe that my purpose in life is to bring a smile to everyone I encounter. Bringing my purposeful self to life – my BEING self at its core – is created through the *intentional* action I bring to each encounter throughout each day. To achieve this, I have adopted a practice of *being intentional* toward this daily goal. My intentional practice to bring a smile to everyone I encounter requires that I 'see' each person; that I acknowledge who they are; that I notice and acknowledge something about them; and that I offer my gift of a smile to each of them! I intentionally (try to) do this, not only at home, at work – but with everyone – the store clerk, my waiter, a neighbor, my friends. I am engaged (fully) in what I believe is important to BEING my best, purposeful self.

Now, back to the race.

As you can easily imagine, for someone who hates to run, when I approached the four-mile mark, my head was filled with all sorts of negative thoughts; thoughts that were convincing me that I couldn't finish and should quit the race. As I approached the line of high school football players handing out the water, I reached out my hand and, ever so routinely, grabbed a cup of water. I said thank you. But then added – "What a pleasure it is to get water from such wonderful, cheerful and encouraging young men!"

As I continued past the line of football players, I heard one of them say – "Did you hear that? She said that right after she looked at me!"

I could hear the smile in his voice. Hearing this, I smiled, and realized that I had created a smile with a person I encountered. I had brought my intention forward in my acknowledgement of their best-self qualities, and I didn't do it with a conscious intention!

I realized that, by being intentional in my practice of bringing a smile to everyone I encountered, I was intentionally BEING my best self and bringing my purpose forward in my actions, attitudes and behaviors. My practice of creating a smile was now an integral part of my BEING. I was BEING how I intended to show up, and it mattered… to me and to the high school football player that lovely Saturday morning.

> By being intentional in my practice, I was intentionally BEING my best self.

How You Show Up Is How They Show Up

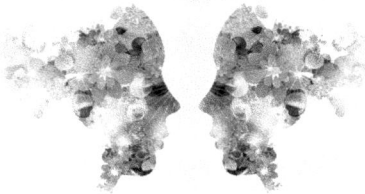

How you show up matters. It matters because, as a leader, through your actions, interactions and ways of BEING, you are the principal influencer of the culture, values and relationships that support the work of each individual. Simply put, how you show up is how they show up. You are the lead orchestrator of the environment. If you want your staff to be kind to others - BE kind. If you want your staff to develop trustworthy relationships - BE trustworthy. If your desired state is one where your staff are smiling and enjoy their work, then smile and love what you do.

**How you show up is
how they show up.**

Taking a minute to reflect on this idea of 'how you show up is how they show up', my brain jumps immediately back to what it was like to work in an environment where my leader led from a place of ego, control and fear versus a place of caring for, supporting and encouraging others. Many of the employees mirrored his behavior, while others were figuring out how to be seen in the organization as productive and valuable and, at the same time, avoid the wrath of his interactions. The environment was always tense, with much of the energy focused on staying out of trouble, instead of leveraging our confidence, competence and talents to positively affect the organizational business objectives. How he showed up is how we showed up - defensive, defeated and drained.

Contrasting this to other work experiences where I had the privilege to work with, and for, leaders who trusted me and encouraged my best self, I recalled how I felt valued, confident, energized and comfortable. Their strengths, characteristics and qualities present in their way of BEING influenced the work environment and directly influenced my way of BEING (aka - how I showed up). As I think about those leaders, these are but a few of the individual characteristics that stood out.

- . - . - . - . - . - . -

Accountable	*Emotionally Intelligent*	*Kind*
Approachable	*Empathic*	*Listens*
Calm	*Engaging*	*Passionate*
Caring	*Genuine*	*Positive*
Collaborative	*Happy / Joyful*	*Respectful*
Committed	*Honest*	*Self-Aware*
Confident	*Humorous*	*Smiles*
Creative	*Inclusive*	*Supportive*
Decisive	*Innovative*	*Trustworthy*
Delegates	*Inspiring*	*Zestful*

- . - . - . - . - . - . -

These leader characteristics and strengths are the intrinsic qualities that have the capacity to directly influence the behaviors of others if we consciously and intentionally choose to bring them forward into our leadership way of BEING.

If This, Then That

How you show up is how they show up was, for me, where the 'rubber meets the road'. If I wanted my staff to create experiences where individuals, colleagues and patients felt respected, understood, cared for, and reassured, then I had to consider shaping those interactions, not by training and telling, but rather by choosing to show up in a way that created the experience first-hand, and gave them an opportunity to connect to the experience in a way that was meaningful to them.

Let's do a metaphorical equation of behavior change. If you want to create human relationships and interactions (patient, family, staff and colleagues) that are caring, empathic, trustworthy, and respectful, then it's important for leaders to BE the same - caring, empathic, trustworthy and respectful. How you show up is how they show up.

Putting the 'then' statement into action can often require a conscious intentionality to BE those qualities and bring them into each interaction. Rarely would an effective leader, one who was interested in influencing the outcome of a meeting, show up without having put some forethought, ahead of time, into the flow of the meeting, what objectives were to be discussed and the expected outcome. To do this, time is set aside to plan an agenda that leads to the desired results. Anticipating questions, bringing clarity to the discussion, paying attention to how people are reacting to what is shared, and what steps are necessary to achieve the desired outcome: all of these influence what actions are taken to support the meeting objectives.

This same planning and intention holds true in how you show up to influence the behaviors of your staff.

Consider creating an intention in how you wish to show up to create an environment that fosters caring, therapeutic relationships between staff, colleagues and patients. Bring clarity to what the presence of leader characteristics looks like in your actions, attitudes and behaviors. Be specific in what words and non-verbal behaviors you choose to incorporate into your leadership way of BEING.

Consider asking yourself these questions.

_._._._._._._._._._.

- *What do I want my staff to experience when connecting with me?*
- *What will I notice in them that is evident of the presence of a specific strength, characteristic or quality?*
- *What is meaningful to me in bringing these leader characteristics to my interactions?*

_._._._._._._._._._.

BE intentional to cultivate your intentional BEING. Notice the impact of your intention. Turn your observer on and calibrate it to notice how your staff are choosing to show up, and acknowledge them, bringing clarity to how their best selves are showing up. Pay attention to how patients, colleagues and co-workers are responding and connect the dots between how you show up and how they show up.

Your conscious awareness of your individual strengths and leadership qualities, together with your deliberate choice to bring these forward in your actions, interactions and way of BEING, influence the actions and interactions your staff have with each other and with their patients and families.

Creating a Person Centric Experience

Whether I'm leading a meeting, coaching a client, delivering a workshop or speaking in front of a group of individuals, I have, as part of my preparation, made a practice to create an intention that brings clarity to how I wish to show up. Saying out loud and writing down my intention to shift my energy from 'it's all about me' to 'it's all about them' creates an authentic experience that is engaging, energizing and enjoyable for the participants. Leading hArtfully is creating a person-centric experience that is all about them (your staff and colleagues) - discovering and acknowledging their best. And, it requires a shift from an ego-centric (self) focus to a person-centric (others) emphasis. And so, I ask myself these questions.

— · — · — · — · — · — · —

- *How do I want to show up to create a person-centric experience?*
- *What do I want them to experience?*
- *What will I look for to know I am showing up in a way that honors and values them?*
- *What energy do I want to bring into the room?*
- *What fears, judgments and assumptions do I need to set aside?*
- *What individual strengths will I draw upon?*

— · — · — · — · — · — · —

Brandon and Mary had both been participating in group coaching sessions - developing their practice of leading hArtfully and choosing to discover the best in others. In one of our sessions, they asked if we could explore how they could best approach a 'difficult conversation' they had scheduled with one of their employees.

Following our practice of inviting discovery, reflection and action to our coaching conversations, we began the discussion with a series of questions that outlined what they wanted the individual to experience during the conversation. Not surprisingly, they shared that they wanted her to feel supported and encouraged. They wanted her to know they valued and appreciated her. They wanted her to feel comfortable to co-create actions that would encourage her best self. They wanted her to know that they cared about her as a person. And, they certainly didn't want her feeling defensive, angry or even shameful.

I often say, 'the burden of change lies with the leader'. It wasn't merely up to the staff member to show up for this crucial conversation, open to alternative approaches and comfortable to participate in a critical discussion - it was up to her leaders to additionally show up in a way that invited trust and influenced the environment to create an open dialogue, where new actions, attitudes and behaviors could be thoughtfully considered.

The burden of change lies with the leader.

Once we outlined the experience they wanted to create, the next step, of course, was to bring clarity to how they could create that. And so we explored how to create the experience.

_._._._._._._._.

- *How would the meeting begin?*
- *What ways could they create a conversation (vs. telling) that opened up a dialogue for discovery?*
- *What energy would they bring into the room?*
- *How would they focus on the details of their concerns, constructively outlining the facts, limiting judgement and justifications?*
- *What questions could they ask to prompt awareness and reflection?*
- *What strengths could be leveraged and acknowledged to reinforce their trust and confidence?*
- *How would they invite alternative choices and actions to co-create productive next steps?*
- *How would they invite accountability and commitment?*
- *How would they offer their support?*

_._._._._._._._.

We closed the discussion by exploring what was important to them about creating a person-centric experience and leading through the heart.

Equipped, prepared and with their intentions clearly defined, they had their crucial conversation with the staff member. Never was there a more perfect example of 'how you show up is how they show up' in what occurred within their meeting and interaction. Not only did they create an environment that fostered trust, honesty and meaningful dialogue, but together they co-created an agreeable, productive plan forward. In the end, the staff member shared her appreciation for the tone of the meeting, the supportive conversation and the opportunity to explore alternatives together. Brandon and May were ecstatic. They witnessed what was possible when they showed up as their best-leader selves and were now enthusiastically empowered to continue to bring forward those actions, attitudes and behaviors to encourage, support and create new potentials. This was confirmed in a post-conversation call, where Mary shared that she was "truly grateful to learn a human and humane leadership style that emphasizes conversation, heart, and positivity!"

VI
THE E'S OF ENGAGEMENT

"The only way to do great work
is to love what you do."

- Steve Jobs

How you show up to influence and cultivate a culture where staff, colleagues and patients feel valued, cared for, and trusted is an essential part of the equation of why it matters how we show up. Our actions, interactions and way of BEING are vital to encouraging individual change and engaging staff in what is meaningful to them - caring for others and making a difference in people's lives.

Engage the Individual

One of my first assignments working in healthcare, was to identify and correct systemic risk issues that resulted in large liability claims within the obstetrics (OB) service line, across a 17-hospital system, I was responsible to lead a team of expert OB and perinatal physicians and nurses, chartered to identify the root and common causes of these claims and then implement and hardwire effective corrective actions to mitigate any occurrence or reoccurrence of the associated risk.

Equipped and skilled in cause analysis, quality improvement and project management methodologies, I felt confident to lead the team forward to define the problem(s) and implement improvement strategies. The efforts of the team would not only result in reducing mortality and injury to patients, but would limit the multi-million dollar financial liability to the organization; two very important strategic objectives.

While each of the clinical team members certainly appreciated the organizational importance of the work we were doing - implementing a large-scale, complex, multifaceted change in practice, workflow, and protocols - I soon learned that simply appreciating how the organization would benefit was not sufficient to achieve the objective. In order to keep the team engaged, present and committed to forging through this ever-so-challenging and time-consuming, important work, I had to figure out how to engage them as individuals in this massive change initiative and to help them find individual and personalized meaningfulness - what was important to them, not the organization - about this call to action.

Defining and designing what we referred to as 'the OB System' required innovative thinking that stretched past the limits of 'this is how we've always done it'. It further required conversation, negotiation, creativity, understanding and respect between team members. The glue that held the team together was trust and a shared sense of purpose. It was time-consuming work, taking more than nine months to complete the cause analysis and another two years to build the clinical protocols and design an electronic decision support system that would later guide and standardize the clinical practice of obstetrics. The work was challenging, exhausting and at times discouraging; but it rarely, however, overshadowed or diminished the meaningfulness, fulfillment and sense of accomplishment we gained from it.

Emphasizing and reinforcing their impassioned shared purpose and mission to make a difference, and deliberately leveraging their clinical expertise and individual strengths that engaged and connected them to this important work, was fundamental to our formula for success. Paying attention to their individual and group energy, frustration levels, lack of understanding and overwhelmed feelings of 'this will never happen', was essential to continued progress. Consistently building into my conversations, presentations and exercises the importance and meaningfulness of the work they were doing was critical. I invited executive leaders to our weekly meetings and three-day working sessions to share their appreciation, encouraging them to continue and connecting their work to the organizational mission. I would invite patients and families to share with the team stories of positive impact to amplify and underscore the importance of their efforts. We watched videos of 'a day in the life' of families where a birth resulted in complications and subsequent lifelong care requirements, reconnecting each individual to their purpose in being part of the team. And I invited their voices, to share their perspective, passion and the significance of their work, and why their participation on this improvement team was meaningful to each of them. I paid attention to how I showed up each day, making sure to bring my best self to them, caring for each individual and consciously bringing those humane qualities of leadership to the forefront.

Every element of these leadership practices was intentional to engage each team member - personally - in the meaningfulness of their labors, consistently aligning their individual contributions with the organizational objectives to improve care and mitigate risk. Maximizing their commitment, connected to the meaningfulness of the work, created the momentum, engagement and focus to achieve our initiative goals, with the liability claims falling to a negligible level.

The experience, along with the validation of the importance of engaging individuals in meaningful change, led me to develop and crystalize a formula for engagement:

$$E's = mC^2$$

Engagement = meaningful Contagious Change

The E's

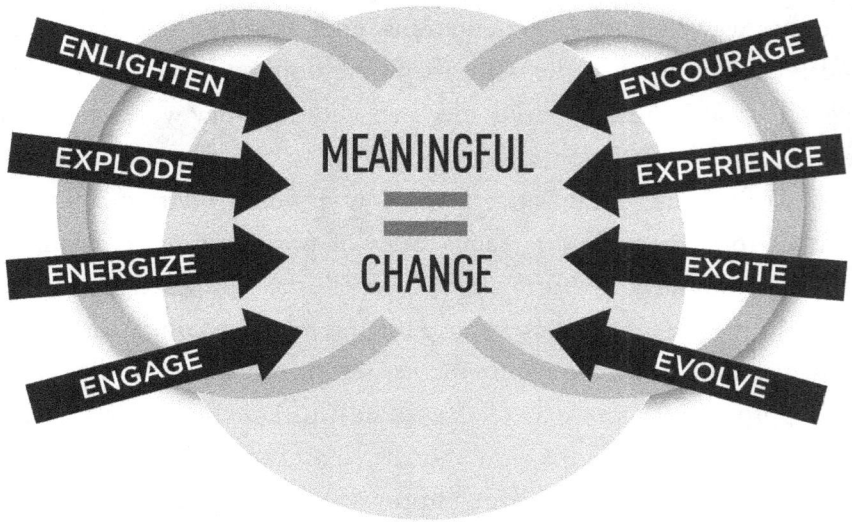

- **Enlighten** with purpose
- **Explode** with passion
- **Energize** with the possibility of a new way
- **Engage** the heart
- **Encourage** at all levels
- **Experience** it - Do it, Feel it, Share it
- **Excite** with enthusiasm
- **Evolve** - Learn, Choose, Do, Reflect

The E's are how you show up to invite meaningful, engaged, individual change.

The E's of engagement are leading hArtfully practices that are integrated into your actions, interactions and way of BEING to create conversations that foster discovery, reflection and subsequent change in employee and colleague actions, attitudes and behaviors. Their use is intended to inspire and motivate, and they are essential to invite shifts from the current state to the desired state. Their presence is deliberate and intentional to create a positive, supportive, encouraging environment where meaningful experiences occur. The E's are how you show up to invite meaningful, engaged, individual change.

Not surprisingly, and consistent with a leading hArtfully way of BEING, putting the E's into practice requires a conscious, thoughtful, intention to adopt a new way of doing and BEING - or as I like to refer to it as - an E-tention. What follows is a description of each E, followed by an invitation to create an E-tention to show up in ways that engage the individual and create a meaningful, contagious change.

Note: Leading this team was one of the most rewarding experiences I had the privilege to be a part of... because the work we were doing mattered... to me. My experience working with the OB team, and the relationships I built set a foundation of magnificence that carries forward within me today. Incredible people doing incredible work that matters; I am forever grateful to have been a part of a team that fundamentally changed clinical practices to ensure the safe delivery of more than 30,000 babies each year.

Enlighten with Purpose

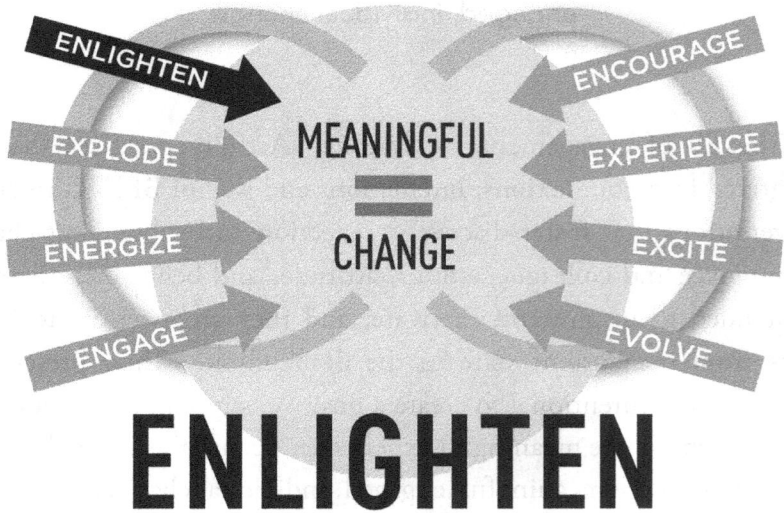

There is much research and literature around the importance of the connection to purposeful work in having an engaged workforce. A quick Google search shows more than 250 million articles outlining the steps, perspectives and effects of connecting to purpose in the workplace. My coaching courses additionally echoed the importance of inviting our clients to discover meaning in their sought-after goals; reinforcing that human beings were 'meaning making' and, through a clear understanding of what was important to them, the hard work of change could occur. Meaningfulness and purpose are not only key to building higher levels of employee engagement, but as Martin Seligman, founder of the field of positive psychology suggests, having a meaningful connection to something greater than ourselves is a crucial element of well-being.

The bottom line is that having a connection to purpose and finding meaning in what we do is important to the productivity, effectiveness and levels of engagement within our teams. And how we show up as leaders each day, to enlighten our employees with a meaningful connection to how what they do matters - matters.

Thinking back to my aircraft industry days in the early 1990's, McDonnell Douglas (now Boeing) had taken on the initiative of Lean Manufacturing. The overall focus of this endeavor was to improve the production quality and efficiency within the aircraft industry. Japanese companies, like Toyota Motor Corporation, led the way in implementing lean practices and demonstrating improved quality and efficiency across their manufacturing operations. Wanting to learn how to incorporate these principles and practices into the McDonnell Douglas production facilities, a multidisciplinary team of engineers, production managers, maintenance technicians and executive leaders visited the Toyota factory in Japan.

When the team returned from their learning expedition, they enthusiastically shared their discoveries with organizational leaders. One of the things that astounded many of the exploratory team members was that any worker on the Toyota production line had the authority to stop production at any time. This was unheard of among the McDonnell production managers, as maintaining schedules and deliveries were paramount. Open to new perspectives, our team learned how each Toyota employee felt individually responsible for the quality of the product and was empowered to ensure it met all requirements. They shared how this practice was not only an organizational policy, but a principle each individual could personally articulate with a meaning for them. Employees understood and valued the importance of their individual responsibilities in producing quality vehicles. They personally connected to ensuring the safety of each driver and passenger. And they shared powerful stories of validation - letters from customers where their commitment to quality was realized. They were personally invested in the work product. This example was a striking difference in how the aerospace industry engaged the workforce to build and deploy commercial and military aircraft.

When I entered the healthcare industry, it was different, but the same. The OB clinical team of nurses and physicians were the key players in delivering quality and safe care to their patients. It was easy to imagine that these clinical care givers would be able to connect to the importance of the lifesaving work they were doing. Yet, somehow in the multitude of processes, tasks, and productivity requirements, this sense of purpose was easily lost. And, to make matters worse, the introduction of the electronic medical record, with its task-oriented way in which care was outlined and documented, made it now more difficult for clinical individuals to be connected to what mattered to them - caring for another human being.

Had it not been for my deep search for purpose, things might have gone differently in how I led my clinical improvement teams. I was certainly comfortable leading the 'mechanics' of improvement initiatives, but with my entrance into healthcare and the opportunity to 'make a difference', I felt a personal responsibility to ensure that each baby was born with the best clinical care and quality outcomes. I had a clear sense of purpose and this strong connection to meaningfulness bled over into my leadership of the OB team. This incredible group of expert obstetric clinicians worked together for two years, designing and creating clinical care plans, weaving in patient stories of why our work was important, and consciously connecting the discrete elements of our efforts to how it mattered to the babies, their parents, their families, and to themselves.

As I transitioned into coaching and shifted my time to working with clinical teams in the emergency department, my conversations and observations consistently uncovered moments when the impact of *their* work was ever so evident. As an observer, I could see how the relationships they created, the empathic way in which they responded to the patients' needs, and their keen ability to listen and validate the patients' emotional message was powerfully impactful. Yet, as mentioned, many of the clinicians were blind to this, their attention and concentration operationally focused on the volume of patients needing medical attention, the challenges of managing multiple patients at a time, and the inefficiencies rooted in the care processes that made it difficult to do and BE their best medical experts.

But, when I shared with them what I noticed in their actions, shining a light on the positive patient impact they were making, it seemed to open up the conversation into how they were helping others and making a difference in peoples' lives; reconnecting them to why they chose to go into healthcare and bringing meaning to their work.

'Enlighten with purpose' creates the dialogue that prompts a response to the question of 'what's important about this to you'?

Leading hArtfully brings the 'E' of Enlighten with Purpose into your leader practices, by creating conversations that uncover what is meaningful to the individual in the work they are doing. In short, 'enlighten with purpose' creates the dialogue that prompts a response to the question of 'what's important about this to you'?

One effective way to begin this conversation is to ask your staff to share a story of a favorite patient encounter. As they are speaking, listen closely for the 'change-a-world moments' they create and then hold up the mirror for them to discover how what they do connects to something meaningful to them.

A recent interview with a group of call center employees uncovered the depth of connection to purpose and shared engagement possible within an organizational setting. These employees have the responsibility to schedule patient appointments with physicians at their clinics; more than 2 million patient interactions are logged each year. When I began my interviews, I expected to hear the employees describe how they expertly and efficiently scheduled patient appointments. Instead, what I heard in their stories was a sincere passion for caring for another human being, building personal relationships with patients and supporting them through their healthcare journeys. Sure, they were able to coordinate the schedules and times to get patients appointments - but, in doing so, they bonded with these patients, listening to them share their experiences, bringing empathy and understanding to each interaction.

When asked what was important about the work they do, they eloquently responded with reflections and patient statements:

- *My patients appreciate the humanness I bring to our interactions*
- *I want our patients to feel like they are talking to someone they know*
- *My patients say it feels like you're holding my hand through the phone*
- *Saving a life is not above and beyond, it's what we do each day*
- *I build trust and offer hope to my patients each day*
- *My conversations with patients are powerful and impactful*
- *I smile through the phone, it makes the patient feel comfortable*
- *Everyone has a story to share - I want to create a space for them to feel heard*
- *Helping patients get to where they need to be is important to me*

Listening to their responses, I realized it wasn't only them that were enlightened. I was overwhelmed with a whole new perspective and now keenly aware of the importance of their work. Sadly, my judgments and invalidated assumptions had gotten in the way of discovering their best selves. They were no longer schedulers, responsible for making appointments; rather, they were remarkable people who were individually responsible for, and committed to, helping patients navigate through their healing journey. Their conversations, filled with empathy, compassion and caring, had the capacity to change a world and, as I held up the mirror for each of them to see their best self, I was additionally enlightened with the importance of their connection to their purpose and the most magnificent way they carried it out.

Within this call center, performance is measured in numbers - counts, seconds and minutes. The visibility of their performance is ever present, with large neon red and green metric indicators - patient wait time, calls on hold, number of transfers - flashing the operational scores across a huge jumbotron throughout the day and pushing them further away from a connection to purpose. Opening up the space and inviting individuals to share and reflect on the impact of their work, invites a conversation that enlightens and connects them with purpose and brings meaning to what they do each day. 'Enlighten with purpose' augments the discussion and puts continuous focus on operational priorities to connect the employee to the meaning behind the performance measure.

> Opening up the space and inviting individuals to share and reflect on the impact of their work, invites a conversation that enlightens with purpose.

Taking the time to create a conversation around purpose, asking individuals what is important to them about the work they do, and connecting their responses to individual and organizational goals, creates new levels of engagement and a sense of accomplishment. Here are some examples of questions that invite enlightened connections to individual purpose.

— · — · — · — : — · — · — · —

- *Why did you go into healthcare?*

- *What brings you joy each day?*

- *What's important to you about the work you do?*

- *How is it you make a difference in the lives of your patients / colleagues?*

- *Tell me about one of your favorite patients or work experiences*

- *At the end of the day, what would you acknowledge yourself for in how you changed a world?*

- *How do you stay connected to what is meaningful to you?*

- *What do you suppose a patient or co-worker might say about you?*

— · — · — · — : — · — · — · —

Create conversations where your staff are invited to share their stories of how they make a difference. Notice how you too, are enlightened - by the depth of meaningfulness and commitment they have in honoring their work responsibilities. Taking the time to explore what is important to the individual opens the door for magnificence to flourish, encouraging their best selves and BEING your best hArtful leader.

Create an E-tention to 'Enlighten with Purpose'

... bringing questions that create meaningful conversations, connected to purpose, to your interactions.

Explode with Passion

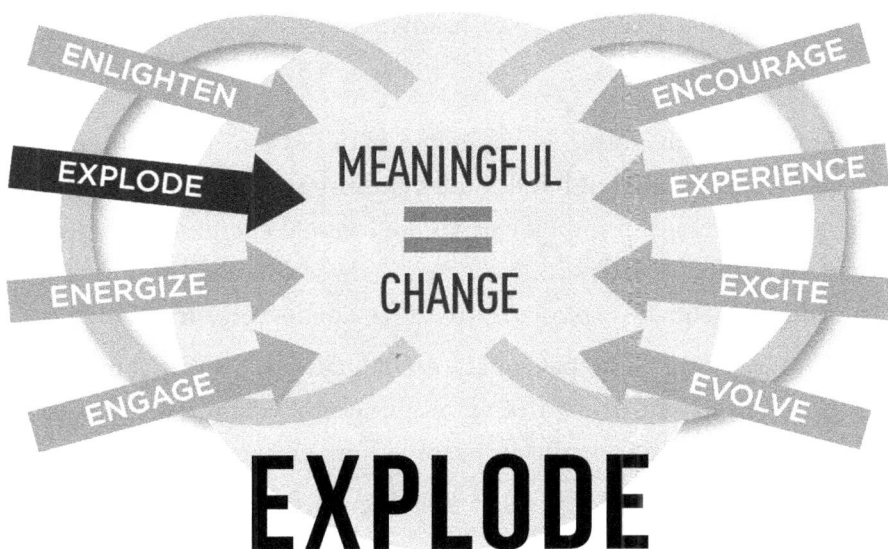

ENLIGHTEN
ENCOURAGE
EXPLODE
EXPERIENCE
ENERGIZE
EXCITE
ENGAGE
EVOLVE

MEANINGFUL
=
CHANGE

EXPLODE

Explode with passion. Each time I think of this 'E', Tigger from Winnie the Pooh immediately jumps into my mind. His external energy and inviting way of BEING is intense and often contagious. He is confident, cheerful and definitive in what he enjoys, and doesn't. His positive energy and emotions affect his behavior and influence those around him.

When I think about people who are passionate, the first word that comes to mind is 'explode'! Their energy is bursting with invitation, drawing you into the conversation with their engaging and expressive language. Their direction is clear, unwavering in its pathway forward and congruent in their actions, attitudes and behaviors. Passion is vital to inspiring, motivating and leading others. It is the energy behind the vision that fuels others to follow, and is the spark that ignites individuals' action.

> Passion is the energy behind
> the vision that fuels others
> to follow.

And while this notion of exploding with passion often conjures up images of powerfully bold and loudly enthusiastic behaviors, passion is also quietly present in individuals whose internal energy and leadership compass, guided by their strong conviction toward something meaningful and valued, is equally explosive in their passionate presence.

But one thing these passionate individuals all have in common, is a connection to something deeply meaningful to them that most often extends beyond their centric self to something greater than themselves.

You might recall from our earlier discussion that I was passionate about equipping clinicians, creating processes and leveraging technology to minimize adverse events related to obstetrical care. This meaningful connection to something greater than myself, fueled my energy, drive and stamina to lead the team forward, overcoming the many challenges we would encounter in implementing a large change initiative. That's the thing about passion - it IS the energy behind what motivates us forward. Of course, there was an organizational vision of what the team was asked to accomplish. And we were very clear in outlining and bringing clarity to those goals and objectives.

But that's not what fueled our individual and team energy with passion. It was the emotionally charged connection to something greater than ourselves: We were working to help every single baby born within that healthcare system to have the opportunity for a full and complete life. We were passionate about offering life. And we felt and experienced the emotion and energy, each of us, of what that new life offered each family. Exploding with passion is more than having excitement toward a goal - it's an emotional connection, and personal attachment to a purpose that makes working hard and achieving the impossible, possible.

This notion of exploding with passion was made ever so clear as a friend of mine, Cathy, shared her experience in being invited to sing Beethoven's 9th Symphony (Ode to Joy) with the Louisville Kentucky Orchestra. She, of course, loves to sing. And is quite good - duh!... She's singing with an orchestra! And, I suppose, on the surface one could assume that she is passionate about singing and even more excited about the opportunity to sing this masterpiece with other extraordinary vocalists. Yet, there was something stronger that enabled the emotional pull to prepare and grind through the rehearsals that warranted a spectacular performance.

Music is a superb example of exploding with passion because it's filled with energy and life. It's bold and soft together, to create tension, movement and connection. It's filled with emotion that takes your breath away and connects individuals to a deeper, meaningful experience beyond hearing a string of notes. Music invites others into a space where their senses are amplified and the quality of the experience intensely palpable. Cathy told me that singing with the orchestra wasn't about performing music; rather, it was, for her, about bringing people closer together, to be one with the performers and to transcend the audience to a higher level of experience... to connect to something greater than themselves.

Exploding with passion brings people together. It's an invitation to step into a space greater than ourselves. It brings 'what matters' into focus. As leaders, we are the stewards of guiding others into that space of 'what matters', influencing the emotional direction of the journey forward.

Dr. Franklin is a radiation oncologist. This is a doctor who treats cancer patients, using radiation as a treatment intervention to help cure or slow the cancer. He is a brilliant doctor, expert in his field and well respected among his clinical colleagues. I had the pleasure of meeting him as part of a physician coaching program being piloted in a large academic hospital. Our first coaching session was scheduled in his office, and, walking in, I was overwhelmed with awe, seeing this space filled with thank you cards. The cards were every color, shape and size you can imagine, taped to every available space within his office. And before the 'formal' coaching conversation even began, he pointed to one of the cards and launched into the story of a grateful patient whose life had changed because of him. With tears in his eyes, he shared with me, not what he did medically to stop the cancer from progressing, but what it meant to him to be able to positively alter the life of a human being - a brother, a son, a husband, a father, a daughter, a sister, a mother, a grandmother. He had invited me into his world of offering hope, life, dreams, and the meaningfulness it had to him. His passion was exploding within our conversation, ever so quietly and personally, and I was connecting to the significance he felt in being part of something greater than himself.

These conversations, the ones that personalized every patient encounter, and connected compassion, comfort and caring for another individual, were constant in his interactions with his residents, staff and colleagues. His personalized passion to offer hope to others was consistently present in the way he led the department and leaked into the way his staff and residents also interacted with patients. Walking through the department, you could hear intimate, personal conversations between the staff and the patients. There was nothing rote or task-oriented to anything about the patient visit. Every element of the patient visit was personalized and personal. His staff had their stories to share as well. And in listening to their stories, quietly unfolding the passion in their voice, their words, their eyes, I was touched by the profound impact each of these people had in caring for another human being.

Dr. Franklin, in his way of BEING, through his actions, attitudes and behaviors, and with an unwavering commitment to travel a pathway lined with stories of change-a-world moments, had left footprints that others wanted to follow. How he showed up, was how they showed up... and it was exponentially explosive in changing multiple worlds.

Create an E-Tention to 'Explode with Passion'

...leaving footprints that others will want to follow.

Energize with the Possibility of a New Way

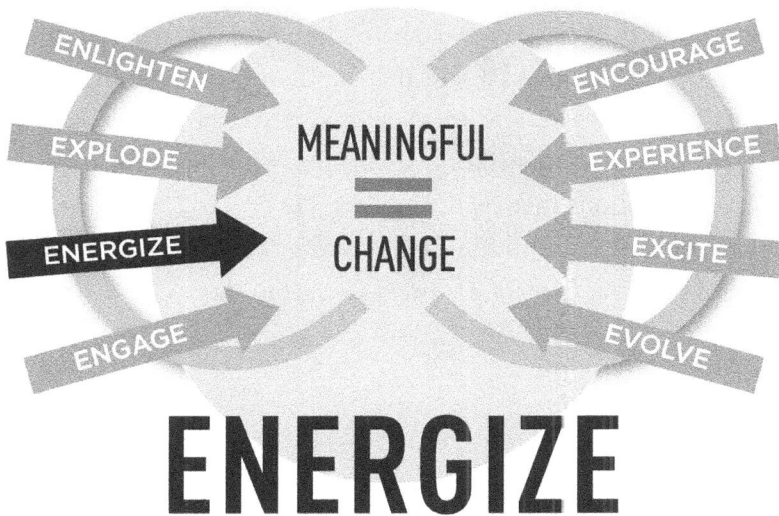

ENLIGHTEN   ENCOURAGE
EXPLODE   EXPERIENCE
ENERGIZE   **MEANINGFUL = CHANGE**   EXCITE
ENGAGE   EVOLVE

ENERGIZE

This 'E' - 'energize the possibility of a new way', may be the most crucial in facilitating change and bringing visibility to the shifts that are occurring from the current state to the desired state. 'Energize with the possibility of a new way' is about taking the time to highlight what happens when a new action, attitude or behavior is tried. When leaders bring this 'E' into the conversation, it clearly connects impact to actions taken. It's as if the leader is enthusiastically walking around with their observer turned on, noticing new ways of doing and BEING and with an energizing tone, saying to the individual - "Did you see that?!?!"

> Bringing this 'E' into the
> conversation clearly connects
> impact to actions taken.

One of my most memorable moments when I energized a client with the possibility of a new way was with Russ. Russ is an emergency medicine certified physician's assistant, working in a high volume, urban emergency room. And before I share the story, let me tell you a bit about Russ. First, it must be said that he is an incredible human being. He is a father, husband, and brother in a very large family. He's one of those guys that everyone likes - always showing up with a smile and creating conversations that spark laughter. He is kind, caring, patient and supportive of those around him. He's confident, skilled and helpful. And the kind of guy that everyone wants to be around.

Meet Russ

The first time I met Russ was in the emergency department. I was scheduled to work with one of his colleagues, doing an observational coaching session. At the time, the observational coaching sessions were part of my *Engaging the hArt*™ workshop series that I delivered to emergency medicine clinical providers. Within the workshop, I introduced and reviewed communication skills and practices focused on building therapeutic relationships with patients. The observational coaching session is a strengths-based approach to observing the presence of those skills and bringing awareness of their associated positive, productive impact to the clinical participant.

I introduced myself to Russ, and was surprised when he immediately responded, saying that he 'already knew me'. With a confused look on my face I asked where we had previously met. He replied - "In your workshop!" Now, with an even more confused look, and questioning my own memory, I told him I didn't remember him being in the workshop. Instantly, he began regurgitating the topics of the workshop to me. Inside my head, I was convinced he had not participated in a workshop, and yet his descriptions of the topics and explanations of their meaning were incredibly accurate. This banter of challenging and confirming his participation lasted for minutes that eked into the teens. In the end, he laughed - we all laughed - as he shared that his 'buddy' had told him all about it. Russ is a guy that likes to play - with you.

Discovering the Best; Uncovering Actions, Attitudes and Behaviors

Eventually, Russ did participate in the workshop and observational coaching experience. During the workshops, we review and explore essential actions, attitudes and behaviors that help to create a relationship between the patient and provider that is therapeutic. This review examines evidence-based communication skills that, when adopted by the clinician, help to support their ability to:

- Make a Connection
- Say Hello
- Create a Conversation
- Put at Ease
- Say Goodbye

For a complete listing of communication skills, refer to Appendix A - Creating Meaningful Connections; Communication Skills / Techniques.

Time is taken to additionally explore the theoretical elements of Carl Rogers' person-centered approach to creating therapeutic interactions. His theory outlines three core conditions and three attitudes that must be present within an encounter to create a relationship that has a good effect on the body and mind, and contributes to a sense of well-BEING. These include:

- Empathy
- Unconditional Positive Regard
- Congruence
- Nonjudgmental Attitude
- Trust
- Respect

This review sets the foundation for the one-on-one observational coaching experience. Working directly with the clinician on the unit, and at the patient's bedside, the focus of the observational coaching sessions is to bring awareness to the clinician of their own actions, attitudes and behaviors (e.g., communication skills and core conditions and attitudes) that promote and positively influence their interactions with patients and colleagues.

The ability to turn your observer on, not only to notice the presence of these skills and practices during the interaction, but to notice what happens when the skills are used, is fundamental to the coaching experience. Highlighting strengths, coupled with a clinician-centered coaching approach, promotes an encouraging and trusting environment designed to activate a conscious awareness of their actions, attitudes and behaviors and pinpointing with clarity and specificity how these influence the encounter.

Essential to the effectiveness of the coaching experience is the ability to identify and label specific actions, attitudes and behaviors, and to highlight how they are executed during the patient encounter. Labeling these, and bringing attention in 'real time' to what is observed, creates the foundation for a coaching conversation that leads to a conscious, intentional incorporation of the observed techniques into their next patient encounter – laying the foundation for empowered, confident, consistent practice.

So how does all of this theoretical and strengths-based approach to change come together? In essence, I go into the patient's room with the clinician, looking and listening for the presence of a communication skill, core condition and / or attitude. I am paying attention to both their verbal and non-verbal modes of communication, and noting the specific details of how these actions, attitudes and behaviors manifest within the encounter.

I capture the exact words within each phrase they use to communicate and then label each of the phrases with an associated communication skill. Through this process, they become discreetly aware of what they said, and what communication skills they used to convey their message.

Table 1 below provides an example of phrases and associated, labeled communication skills.

PHRASE	COMMUNICATION SKILL
MAKE A CONNECTION	
I would like to...	Personalizes
May I listen to your heart?	Asks Permission
How are you?	Courteous/Polite
I'm sorry to keep you waiting	Apologizes
SAY 'HELLO'	
My name is Alison; and who do you have with you?	Introductions - With Patient/Family
Hell Mrs._____	Refers to the Patient by Name
I understand you are her for chest pain	Familiar with Patient History
CREATE THE CONVERSATION	
What medications work best for you?	Involves the Patient; Asking for Input
You mentioned you were...	Repeats Back Patient's Words
The x-ray results should take about 2 hours	Sets/Manages Expectations
We will do some blood test to better understand...	Explanations - What & Why
Summarizing the plan of care, we will...	Summarizes All Things Discussed
What is your understanding of what to watch for?	Validates Understanding
PUT AT EASE	
Were the pain medications we gave you effective...	Manages Pain
Everything looks really great. Your tests are...	Reassures
That sounds really hard	Empathetic
Dr._____is the cardiologist I am referring you to	Continuity of Care
He's an excellent physician	Manages Up
SAY GOOD-BYE	
Does this sound like a plan that works for you?	Comes to Agreement
I can't give you... but can give you...	Offers Alternatives
what questions do you have for me?	Asks for Questions

Identifying their words brings credibility to the process and provides an individual, personalized assessment of the components within the interaction, reinforcing how they are creating positive, productive, therapeutic interactions through their actions, attitudes and behaviors.

Discovering the Best; Shining a Light on Strengths, Characteristics and Qualities

As part of the observational coaching session, I am also observing the individual's way of BEING; uncovering and shining a light on their unique strengths, characteristics and qualities they have chosen to bring into the patient encounter.

Martin E.P. Seligman and Christopher Peterson, both distinguished psychologists, identified through intensive research, 6 virtues and 24 associated strengths that define those virtues, to describe good, moral character. These character strengths are the core of who we are; the basic elements of our identity - our way of BEING - that help us function at our best, and when used and developed, contribute to well-BEING. (Reference Appendix B, VIA Classification of Character Strengths and Virtues).

Essential to revealing an individual's way of BEING is the ability to identify, and bring visibility to, defined character strengths, and associate the impact of their presence. For example:

- *Were they kind?*
- *Were they confident?*
- *How was their character strength of creativity present in the interaction?*
- *Was their energy inviting conversation?*
- *How did they enter the room... cheerful, open-minded, present?*

With my observer hyper-sensitized and additionally calibrated toward the patient, I am noting how they are responding, both verbally and non-verbally to the interaction. Bringing visibility to the patient's response is crucial to energizing the possibility of a new way, as this is the information that answers the question of 'Did you see that?' It ties the resultant response to the new phrase, the new way of BEING, or the new action, attitude or behavior that is attempted. This is what 'connects the dots' to what was tried, what happened, and what now motivates and energizes the possibility of new ways of doing and BEING.

Opening up to new ways of doing and BEING can make us feel vulnerable, exposed, self-conscious and uncomfortable. So, awareness of what is meaningful, impactful and possible becomes important. Energizing the possibility of a new way builds confidence and invites change by identifying, acknowledging and leveraging strengths, opening up and expanding their choices of possible new ways of BEING, new practices, and new experiences.

> Energizing the possibility of
> a new way builds confidence
> and invites change.

Meet Russ - Again

I was scheduled to observe Russ one late Friday afternoon. It was another very busy day, filled with waiting patients and caring clinicians in the emergency department. One of the first patients that he was scheduled to see was a psych patient. Patients being admitted to the behavioral health unit must enter through the emergency department to be medically cleared - making sure there are no clinical or medical issues that should first be addressed. Psych patients at this facility are gowned in purple scrubs for identification purposes and are generally given a quick head-to-toe assessment.

Wanting to spark his on-purpose awareness and trigger his choice to adopt new ways of interacting, I turned to Russ and said - "Don't forget to turn your observer on." We entered the room, and sitting on the bed was a twenty-something year-old woman, gowned in purple scrubs. She was in the tightest fetal position that I had ever seen. It was difficult to see the patient's face, given her position, but it was evident that she was struggling to be comfortable, and appeared that she certainly didn't want to be in the emergency room.

Russ began the interaction, introducing himself and asking who she had brought with her. She introduced Russ to her husband, whom she referred to as 'that'. Russ sat down and, very quietly, meeting her where she was at, began to talk to her. He immediately recognized her uncomfortableness with her husband's presence, so he kindly asked 'that' to leave the room. And although his questions were purposeful in understanding her medical condition, there was a genuine, caring reassurance about them. He personalized the interaction, smiling and bringing a calm tone to the conversation. He took his time, slowly inviting her into this space of connectivity, and as he did, she began to trust him and open up - figuratively and literally. She told him that Medicaid had once again changed her medication plan, and that all she wanted was to feel 'normal' again. Russ acknowledged that he could help, and empathized with how difficult this must be for her.

Visibly, her demeanor and presence began to change as she became more and more comfortable with him and the conversation. Slowly her arms came unlocked around her knees, as she began to open up. Her long blonde hair was now evident and beautiful against the purple backdrop of color. Her posture straightened as her conversation gained confidence. And I remember thinking how beautiful she was and that her smile brilliantly lit up the room.

This shift in energy was shared by Russ. He was smiling and engaged in the conversation, dancing alongside her as they, together, agreed to medically clear her, and move her to the behavioral health unit.

As we walked out of the room, I turned to Russ and said – "Did you see that?"

Now, most of the time when I ask an individual if they noticed something in the interaction, I generally get the 'Did I see what?" response. But not today. Russ turned to me grinning from ear to ear, and with a certain decisiveness and joy said – *"Did I see that? I made it happen!"*

Russ had turned his observer on and consciously and intentionally brought his best way of doing and BEING into the interaction. His actions, attitudes and behaviors, coupled with his unique characteristics and strengths had created a change-a-world moment… and he knew it.

Facilitating Awareness & Choice

Energizing with the possibility of a new way is enabled by bringing awareness to the individual of what might be possible. This awareness expands the choices of possibility and leads us further toward a desired state. This notion of expanding choices through awareness is a fundamental principle in coaching and showed up in our conversations.

Russ's awareness of his ability to create a different kind of interaction - a new way of doing and BEING was brought about through coaching conversations we had before and after entering the room. Grounded in curiosity and wonder, I asked Russ questions that explored and prompted clarity to what he wanted to bring to each of his interactions. Through these conversations, we pulled back the covers of his strengths and the skills he wanted to leverage to create his 'desired state' interaction. As I acknowledged the presence of these in previous interactions, he gained further trust and confidence in his capabilities, becoming empowered and energized with the possibility of a new way.

These are some questions that invite energy into the possibility of a new way.

– · – · – · – · – · – · –

- *What did you notice to be different in your interaction?*
- *What intention did you create to prompt new actions, attitudes and behaviors?*
- *What sparked energy in your new way of BEING?*
- *What might be possible if you were to bring these actions, attitudes and behaviors forward further into your practice?*
- *What strengths, characteristics and qualities did you leverage forward to create the impact you noticed?*
- *What do you want to do more of?*
- *What made it possible to bring a new way of BEING forward?*

– · – · – · – · – · – · –

Create an E-Tention to 'Energize with the Possibility of a New Way'

... bringing awareness to what is meaningful, impactful and possible when new ways of doing and BEING are attempted.

Engage the Heart

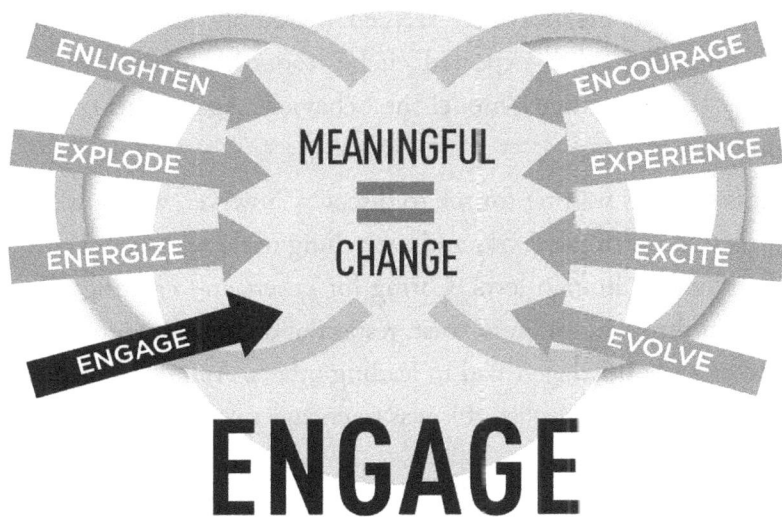

ENLIGHTEN
ENCOURAGE
EXPLODE
EXPERIENCE
ENERGIZE
EXCITE
ENGAGE
EVOLVE

MEANINGFUL = CHANGE

ENGAGE

Many years ago, when I first began working in healthcare, I remember an executive leadership meeting I participated in during my first week at the hospital. As a new employee, I was there to listen and learn. As I sat at the table, listening to their interactions and status updates, I was struck by the way in which the healthcare professionals communicated with each other. They were respectful, kind, and interested in what their colleagues had to say. There was a calmness threaded through the interaction. And what stood out boldly, was how encouraging and supportive they were of each other. I walked out of that meeting room thinking that they cared, truly cared, for each other - at the heart level.

This feeling of caring was a striking difference from what I was accustomed to in the military aircraft industry, where orders were barked and dissatisfaction with employee performance was voiced loudly and continuously. The environment was certainly different.

This notion of caring for others kept coming back to me, particularly as I was developing my new way of leadership BEING. Caring for those that reported to me not only seemed incredibly important, but was quietly consistent with expected cliché leadership approaches - 'walk the talk', 'be the change', 'model the behavior'. Again, this concept was certainly not new.

Yet, what was waiting for me to discover, however, was how this, too, had little to do with the work, and everything to do with how I connected at the individual human level. Caring for others and creating a personal connection through kindness, trust, respect and empathy seemed essential to honoring the privilege I had in leading others. And, it seemed that the only way I could accomplish this was to engage my heart.

I had to completely trust that, by engaging my heart, I could still lead effectively.

To do this, I had to find the courage and conviction to be different from how I thought I should 'show up' in my role as a leader. Adopting a new way of BEING that fostered caring at the heart level required me to change the conduct rules I had made up for myself. It required a new image of leadership and a drastic shift in defined effective behaviors I had witnessed and modeled in the past. It meant, for me, that I had to completely trust that, by engaging my heart, I could still lead effectively to meet the organizational goals and leadership charter. I know how silly that sounds. But, at the time, it seemed nearly impossible for me to genuinely care for people and still get them to do the work that needed to get done. So much had to change within me to make that happen.

BE your Best Authentic Self

It's fair to say that, over time, I had lost my way in BEING my best self as a leader. In fact, many of my leader behaviors were learned, modeled after others, and not intrinsically connected to, nor congruent with, who I was as an individual. If asked to describe myself, I would easily and confidently articulate a mountain of skills - organizer, problem-solver, implementer, team-builder, facilitator, and project manager - never considering that how I showed up as a person each day, and connected with others as a human being, would matter most in influencing the work environment, performance and relationships. And, I certainly never anticipated that choosing to show up as my most human, authentic best self would alter my life so powerfully.

Discovering my best self and trusting that I could lead through my heart, was certainly unfamiliar, foreign and frankly, frightening. I no longer had a sense of who I was as my best authentic self, and I couldn't consciously appreciate what strengths, characteristics and qualities I held within me that positively impacted others. Without this awareness, it was extraordinarily difficult to engage my heart and to care for others.

However, committed to this personal growth exploration, I started paying close attention to what caring for another human being felt like. I asked myself - 'What do I experience when people care about me?' Not surprisingly, I experienced validation that I mattered. I felt I was visible and listened to. I felt supported. I smiled and laughed when I was around people who cared about me. People who cared about me made it easy for me to be my best self in my most natural and authentic way. People who cared about me accepted me for who I was - completely. And, people who cared about me were kind.

Being kind kick-started my focused re-discovery of my best self. I chose to consciously and intentionally bring kindness into each of my personal encounters. I turned my observer on and paid attention to notice what happened in my relationships when I was kind. I observed how having kindness in my heart opened up the floodgates of awareness and access to my individual character strengths, which shifted my motivation to appreciate the significance of the best in me. And when I could begin to see the best in me, I could begin to see the best in others.

This shift and motivation in how I saw myself, also helped to recalibrate what strengths and qualities I looked for in other caring, encouraging, supportive leaders. Surprisingly, what I discovered was their keen ability to simply BE themselves. They were showing up as their authentic, genuine selves, skilled in leading others. I had it backwards. I was trying to BE a leader without the foundation of my authentic best self. BEING me, and bringing my unique best-self strengths and characteristics forward, enabled me to BE a caring, encouraging, supportive leader, showing up in a way that was comfortable, competent and visibly confident.

Engage the Heart of Others

Engaging the heart changed how I chose to show up to work each day. I was no longer a leader who blended into the defined leader genre of the organization, but a colorful, cheerful, energetic, positive, kind, and loving individual in a leadership role. An individual who, each day, could choose to bring a smile to everyone I encountered. This shift was not easy. And I often second-guessed this choice, falling back on more directive and dismissive behaviors. But my conscious, 'on-purpose' awareness of my effectiveness when leading through the heart, and intense connection to why this was important to me, continued to fuel my intention to change my leadership presence.

Engaging the heart brings purpose, meaning and emotion to our actions and relationships. It nurtures an environment where we care for each other. Helping others to engage their heart, to discover and BE their best selves is a critical element of the leader role.

Creating a practice to hold up the mirror to their magnificence, underscoring their individual strengths, characteristics and qualities is, today, a common practice. Helping individuals to see their best self is embedded fluidly in my conversations. I am intentional in turning my observer on and listening for examples of their actions that personify a best-self quality, bringing visibility of these to them through an acknowledgement. And often, my conversations continue, exploring with them the meaningfulness of their actions and the positive impact they had in choosing to bring them forward.

Changing the conversation to engage the heart, BEING my best self to discover the best in others profoundly changed the way I lead, and was visibly appreciated and valued by those I interacted with. I had discovered fulfillment alongside effectiveness as a leader.

Create an E-Tention to 'Engage the Heart'

... BEING your best self to discover the best in others.

Encourage At All Levels

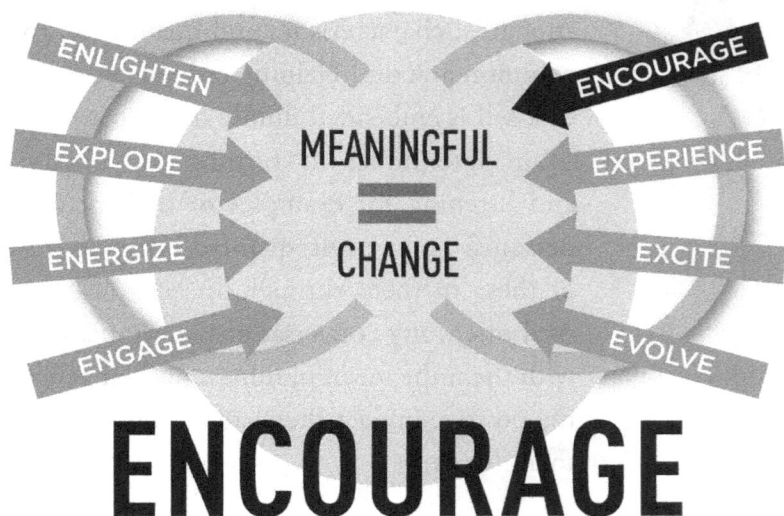

ENLIGHTEN
EXPLODE
ENERGIZE
ENGAGE

MEANINGFUL
=
CHANGE

ENCOURAGE
EXPERIENCE
EXCITE
EVOLVE

ENCOURAGE

What immediately comes to mind when I think about this 'E' is how difficult it can sometimes be to consider *encouraging* people to do what they 'should be doing'. Time and time again, I hear in my coaching conversations that; "Employees are hired to do a job, to perform at a certain level, and to think critically to develop solutions. So why is it that, as a leader, I should encourage them? It's their job!"

Hard to believe, and even more difficult to write, I too in the past, had created in my mind a sort of 'invisible performance threshold' that only I was privy to. And, only when an employee had gone above and beyond that threshold, believed they were entitled to my encouragement and recognition. Even as I write, my brain is thinking… seriously? How is it that I could be so arrogant and egotistical in this reasoning? Could my closed-minded practice of consistently presuming what they 'should be doing', be any more disrespectful and uncaring? As uncomfortable as this leadership reality might feel, and certainly arguably unproductive in motivating and encouraging sustained exceptional performance, time and time again I hear from leaders these perspectives and witness these behaviors.

To encourage at all levels requires a massive shift in mindset, attitude and action. At its core, encouraging at all levels, is believing that each individual has within them the capacity to do and BE their best self. And that they are doing the best they can to bring their best self forward each day. This is foundational to leading hArtfully and consistent with an effective coaching way of BEING.

The Shoulds and Should Nots

When I set the 'it's their job' mentality aside, and connect to what brings me joy in leading others, it becomes quite clear that helping others to reach their fullest potential, bringing forward my most authentic best self - energetic, cheerful, kind, and encouraging - is an important component of my desired leadership state. I am energized by the individuals' faces that light up when they see me enthusiastically cheer them on. I am elated when they appreciate my confidence in them, evidenced in how I hold up the mirror to their magnificence or by my words of 'keep it up, you're doing great'. Who knew that these moments of authenticity could be so meaningful, powerful and impactful... to me?

So, if I am aware of what I positively experience when I am my most encouraging self, then what keeps me from bringing this 'E' into my leader practice on a consistent basis? Judgements. Yep, my own judgements and conditions that I established as expectations of what others *should and should not* meet. These conditions - the shoulds and shouldn'ts - get in our way of creating meaningful, therapeutic relationships and keep us from accepting and acknowledging each individual as doing the best that they can at that moment. It's the shoulds and shouldn'ts that get in the way of offering unconditional positive regard and encouraging at all levels.

You Might Be Surprised - Again

I am so very often surprised at how quick I am to judge. Even more so, how my assumptions and judgements, that I have 'made up in my head', are incorrect. Even today, I was replying to an email where a colleague was sharing how she had adopted a new approach to a project she was leading. Of course, as I was reading the email, I was conscious to encourage and acknowledge this new behavior in my reply, yet I couldn't move past what I noticed to be a missing component. I started my reply acknowledging the adoption of her new way of BEING, and held up the mirror to what I noticed to be impactful. Then, I carefully wove into my reply what I thought she should have also considered. Really?!?!?! I was disturbed, and ever so disappointed, at how I could not let go of my own perspective and control, to trust that she was doing what was most effective for her, her team and the organization.

As I struggled to hit 'Send', realizing that I was more concerned about what I thought she should have done, I paged down to where the email conversation began and noticed, embedded in an earlier message that she had done just what I thought she should have. It was clear in that moment that my judgments were not only inappropriate, but also inaccurate. I had disregarded the practice of believing that each individual has the capacity to do and BE their best and, in doing so, missed the opportunity to fully acknowledge and encourage a colleague.

I did not trust or encourage her to reach her fullest potential. Letting go of those shoulds and shouldn'ts can definitely be difficult. Still today, with an intention to encourage, I am surprised at how often I find the shoulds and shouldn'ts integrated into my conversations. Equally surprising is my awareness of what is possible when I trust that each individual has the capacity to do and BE their best.

Encouraging at all levels invites us to set aside our personal judgements and those conditions of behavior we place on others, and to turn our observer on with a conscious intention to discover the best in others.

Providing support and promoting confidence is the essence of 'encourage'. It inspires courage, fosters hope, and strengthens trust. Imagine what might be inspired, promoted or fostered if you created an intention and then committed to communicate only encouraging statements to your staff?

Notice first, right now, your reaction to that intention.

- *Is this intention and commitment reasonable and feasible?*
- *Is it aligned with your present way of BEING?*
- *Can you outline a clear reason for taking on this commitment?*
- *What might get in the way of bringing this forward?*
- *Can you envision being an effective leader, meeting organization objectives with this being a consistent practice?*
- *How might you leave work each day having brought forward your most encouraging self?*

— · — · — · — · — · — · — · —

Take a moment to bring clarity to how you wish to show up in adopting this practice. Imagine you are walking through your workplace halls with a huge smile on your face and palpable positive energy. You say hello to *each* individual you encounter, and add an encouraging acknowledgement to your greeting.

Here are some examples of acknowledgments that encourage at all levels.

- - · - · - · - · - · - · -

- *Good morning Mary. I see that you are already checking in on Mrs. _____. I bet she was thrilled to see you first thing in the morning!*

- *Hello Alice. Thanks for cleaning up that mess we made last night in room 3. There was so much going on I didn't even notice how bad it was until I saw you emptying the trash!*

- *Hey Joe. Good Evening. Thanks so much for coming in on such short notice. I hate to bother you on your day off. I'll keep an eye on how we are doing tonight and if we catch a break, you'll be the first to go home.*

- *OMG Fred! I stopped by Mr. _____'s room and he let me know that once again you've got the whiteboard up to date with all of his information. He's one of your biggest fans, as I am as well.*

- - · - · - · - · - · - · -

I know, I can already hear you saying - 'I do that'. Yes, I imagine you do. So, let's do more of it - with a focused intensity and consistently for three consecutive days. Encourage at ALL levels - every single individual - acknowledging each of them for doing what they 'should be doing'.

Feed Forward not Feedback

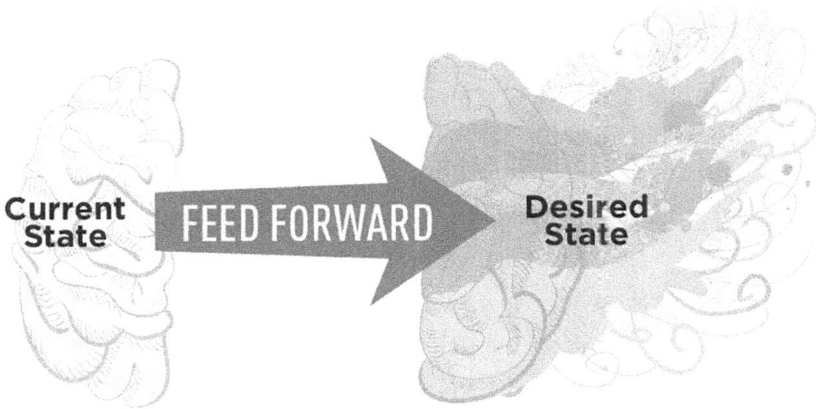

Encouraging at all levels and discovering the best in others additionally demands a shift in mindset and action from giving feedback to feeding forward and empowering your employees to be their best selves.

Feed forward, not feedback. I first heard this concept of feeding forward from the CEO of a large, urban hospital. She and I were brainstorming ideas on how to improve the patient experience, when she used this phrase in a sentence. Immediately it caught my attention.

Hearing these words conjured up two distinct images. Feeding back, or rather, giving feedback, creates images of opposing ideas, withdrawal, and defensiveness. Feeding forward feels collaborative, positive, supportive… and encouraging.

Curious about this idea of feeding forward vs. feeding back, I also looked up feedback in the dictionary. It is defined as 'the output returning to the input'. The definition itself, validated that with feedback, there is no forward movement - *returning to the input*. Yet, we consistently use feedback as the go-to leader tool to promote forward movement and improved performance.

With feedback, there is no
forward movement.

Consider feedback in the context of an audio system. When the sound from the speaker (output) returns to the microphone (input) we hear the feedback... that high-pitched, I-can't-stand-to-be-in-the-room noise. We are compelled to run away from it. And I dare say, it's quite possible that, when we are giving feedback to our employees and colleagues, they too, are compelled to run away. Worse, continuous feedback actually damages the sound speaker; it will render it ineffective in amplifying the sound. And, because of the outer shell design, there is no visible indicator that it is damaged.

This is a powerful metaphor to what could be happening, albeit with good intention, when we are providing continuous feedback; the recipients of our output are potentially made ineffective, with a degree of damage not visible. This perspective presents a strong motivation to consider feeding forward and to engage the heart in your leadership practices, caring for each individual and encouraging their best self.

Perhaps the most common question about this 'E' is - "Do you mean encourage everyone... even those that consistently don't perform at their best?" My response is always 'yes, everyone'... to start. As leaders, we are not responsible for how others choose to show up - but we are responsible to create an environment that fosters new levels of potential and well-BEING. And stepping into this space helps to create that.

Aligned with the belief that each individual has the capacity to do and BE their best, this practice of encouraging at all levels is a tangible step toward inviting the shift in mindset necessary to fully adopt this belief, as it opens up the space for new observations and awareness. The shift can be difficult for sure - setting aside our assumptions, judgments and pride and moving through the uncomfortableness to bring this practice forward. Yet, noticing the uncomfortableness is a superb mental trigger to reflect on the importance of this practice to you, inviting the question of possibility and imagining the experience you create when accessing your superpower to make everyone un-invisible.

With this in mind, coupled with wanting to be a leader committed to caring for and discovering the best in others, the pathway and actions for the next step forward become clear. Armed with your capacity to change a world, consider choosing to encourage at all levels, calibrating your observer to see the magnificence within each individual and offer an acknowledgement.

Shift your leader practices from giving feedback to feeding forward, creating a conversation that nurtures and feeds the individual with fuel that catapults them to the next level of performance. Nourish their creativity and bolster their confidence. Feed their desire to make a difference, fostering new levels of potential and helping them to connect to what is meaningful, purposeful and passionate to them.

Create an E-Tention to 'Encourage at All Levels'

... creating conversations that feed forward, fostering new levels of potential and well-BEING in everyone.

It should be noted that this practice of encouraging at all levels is not a magic potion to facilitate change in each individual's behavior. Everyone has their own capacity to choose how they wish to show up and how they wish to respond. In some cases, alternative approaches to motivation and performance may be required. (E.g., performance management, crucial conversations, etc.).

Experience - Do It, Feel It, BE It

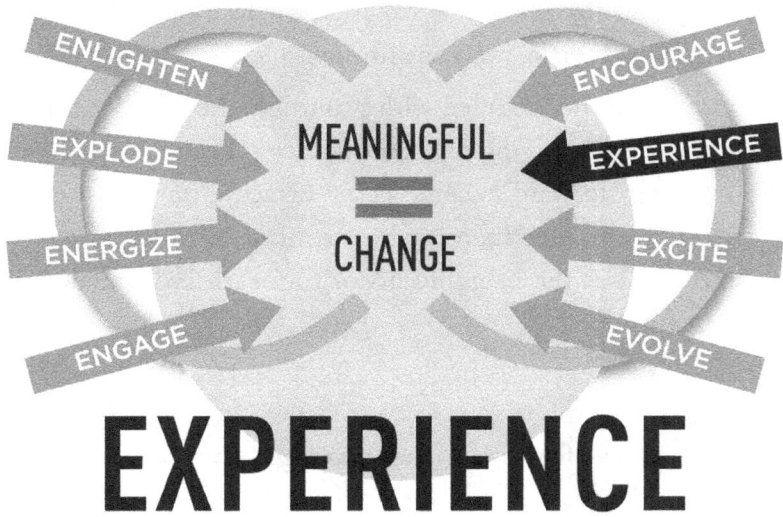

How you show up to influence how they show up gets to the core of this 'E'. 'Experience' consciously appreciates the choice, effort and impact of adopting new ways of doing and BEING, which are only available when we step into change with an intention to understand the experience of change. This 'E' invites action and reflection that guides you in leading meaningful change in an effective, understanding way that values, respects and appreciates those who are participating in a work or life change. This 'E' is connected less to the change itself - the actual modification in how something is achieved - and more to the individual personal experiences and emotions associated with the challenges and accomplishments in shifting from the current state to the desired state. This 'E' is about appreciating the fear, the anxiety, the caution and the courage connected to something new and appreciating the exhilaration and confidence in the accomplishment. And within this 'E', what's behind the 'how we show up' equation - our actions, interactions and way of BEING is an essential consideration in encouraging individual change and engaging staff in what is meaningful to them - caring for others / making a difference.

You Can't Coach What You Don't Experience

This notion of experience is particularly reminiscent of a coaching continuing education class I took with Catherine Morisset, a certified coach specializing in building resilience. During one of her course sessions, she shared - "You can't coach what you don't experience, commit to or apply" - and wow, did that hit home with the meaning of this 'E'. Her quote immediately sparked vivid images and a visceral emotional response of a coaching session that I participated in during my first week of coach certification training that underscores the vital importance of Experience.

I distinctly recall being in that classroom, as if it were yesterday. The tables were set in a semi-circle, with name tents propped at the front of each chair, inviting the impending transformation from complete strangers to supportive coach colleagues. I was uncomfortable, to say the least, hearing my 'inner critic' screaming in my head and listing every reason why I didn't belong in that room, with this elite group of coach wannabes. I felt like a kindergartener at her first day of school - insecure, anxious, timid, and fearful, hoping for the day to end quickly.

The experiential learning model of our training included lectures, coaching application and being coached. The lectures introduced the theory, science, and process of coaching; the coaching application was intended to put the process of coaching into action by practicing coaching each other; and being coached was an observational exercise where we watched an expert coach one of the wannabe coaches from the class. The coaching application and exercises in being coached were extremely uncomfortable, completely foreign and steeped with vulnerability, and so I was surprised when I found myself raising my hand to volunteer to be coached.

I took my seat at the front of the room directly across from the expert coach. We were facing each other - knee to knee, eye to eye. The coach wannabes were seated at the tables surrounding my chair, as if at a campfire storytelling session - only it felt like I was in the center of the fire. The coaching process began with the expert coach asking me if there was anything that I would like to be coached on. I sat for a moment, and then shared an area of my life where I envisioned a new desired state. Talk about diving into the deep end of the exposed, vulnerable, and personal pool! And while I don't recall the topic, I do recall the *experience* of being coached. It was emotional. I remember sitting in that chair, answering the expert's questions thoughtfully and honestly. My responses were quiet and slow to come forward, not sure yet of the level of trust I had with the expert and the observing wannabe coaches. There was an integrity to my responses. I was sincere in my replies. And, I cried. I sat in that chair and cried, her questions cutting ever so deeply into the meaningfulness and importance of why I wanted a change, and at the same time uncovering and realizing my own ability to make that change. It was a powerful moment that brought clarity and action to what I would choose to do to create a shift from my current state to my, now possible, desired state.

In that session, I experienced what it was to be coached. I felt exposed, and at the same time, enlightened with new possibilities. And I remember thinking how surprised I was to have trusted the expert coach enough to share my truest thoughts. Today, as I reflect on that moment, and in my appreciation of BEING a coach, I understand the imperative nature of that trust and how that relationship was formed.

Throughout our coaching conversation, the expert coach consistently acknowledged me, holding up the mirror to my strengths, and uncovering the meaningfulness of my new discoveries, feeding forward my ability to achieve my desired state. There was never any arrogance or judgement in her tone or questions. I believed, and heard in her voice, that she really did want the best for me. It was almost as if there was this force field of trust, filled with energy of support and acknowledgement that buoyed me up and kept me safe within the deep end of this personal pool.

That experience was profoundly impactful. The experience, still fresh in my mind many years later, guides my coaching practice today. It sets a foundation of trust, support and acknowledgement that I consciously and intentionally bring, not only to my clients, but to most of my everyday interactions. That experience shaped how I show up as a coach, and continues to shape how I show up each day, empowered to BE my best self, with my observer turned on to notice and acknowledge the best in others.

Do it, Feel it, and BE it

This notion of trust and the sacredness of the coaching relationship continues to have a strong presence in my coaching practice and individual way of BEING. Creating trust within my coaching client relationships is foundational. And, similar to that moment when I dove into the deep end of the personal pool, there was another moment of experience clarity, where all of the dots within my coach training and practice came together and connected. It was during a specific client relationship where I understood the meaning of what Catherine had shared... you can't coach what you don't experience, commit to or apply... you have to do it, feel it and BE it.

My client was a physician. He was tired of the physical and emotional challenges brought on by his schedule, patient volumes, and workflow inefficiencies and struggling to find joy and fulfillment in caring for his patients. The ubiquitous difficulties within the healthcare work environment and the increasing organizational demands were taking their toll and he found it difficult to connect to his purpose and choice in being a physician. His leadership responsibilities, while important to his professional growth, were additionally time-consuming and put him on a path of new learning and development that triggered his inner critic and questioned his confidence and capabilities. He valued the importance of enhancing the patient experience, yet consistently achieving high satisfaction scores from every patient, every time, proved challenging and felt out of reach.

You can't coach what you
don't experience, commit to
or apply... you have to do it,
feel it and BE it.

He was familiar with my strengths-based coaching approach, and reached out to see if he could benefit from a coaching relationship. Over the course of multiple months, we explored together in detail, and in conversation, what he valued and how these values manifested and connected to his work as a physician. Most importantly, we opened up the conversation to reveal the importance of, and meaningfulness in, what he wanted to bring into his life with his family.

The focus of our coaching conversations began with his desire to improve the patient / physician interaction. He defined his desired state, bringing clarity to what actions, attitudes and behaviors he wanted present in his patient encounters. And he described what he wanted his patients to experience within the interaction. As I listened, threads of clarity and meaningfulness were unraveling within the conversation. And, as I pulled on these through my questions, prompting discovery and reflection, his idea of life's fulfillment was now attainably clear.

Over time, our relationship continued to develop, with the trust between us deepening. Our conversations shifted from specific work situations to broader, more meaningful, personal, life-altering topics. His openness and honesty were sincere and powerful in opening up the space for change. Battling his inner critic, and the voices of the societal 'responsible people' was real and often inconsistent with his desired state. His confidence to step into new ways of doing and BEING was often tenuous. Yet, his vision of what he wanted for himself and his family was crystal clear, which set his compass direction and motivational energy to conquer any obstacles in front of him.

It was his vulnerability and courage to share his most imperfect, authentic self that catapulted my coaching practice to a deeper personal, supportive, and caring level. His exposed openness and brave choice to do the work to move toward his desired state, helped me to show up with my heart engaged, and my ego and pre-supposed expertise 'checked' at the door. Our conversations many times mirrored the experience I had that day I dove into the deep end of the personal pool; only it was he that was now swimming in the pool of discovery. And remembering what that experience felt like for me - feeling exposed, vulnerable, unsure, and scared - confirmed and reinforced my commitment to BE the coach that truly wanted the best for him, and to show up in a way that supported and encouraged him forward. Through our coaching conversations, I consistently acknowledged his progress, connecting his awareness and actions to his desired state, and held up the mirror to those strengths that bolstered his confidence and trust in self to continue. I was conscious of my tone, and regularly created an intention to bring my best, non-judgmental, coaching self to each session.

Reflecting on the many sessions we shared together, it was clear that my experience in coaching him paved the way to apply those same strengths and qualities that my expert coach brought to her coaching that first day of training when I chose to raise my hand. It was through my awareness of my own experience, and the awe of watching my client take giant steps toward a better life, that I realized how to BE a coach and to coach. "You can't coach what you don't experience, commit to, or apply" - it now made so much sense. I couldn't BE a good coach to anyone - ever - until I experienced what it was like to be coached, committed to the practice of discovering the best in others, and applied those actions, attitudes and behaviors I experienced in being coached. Do it, Feel it, BE it - my mantra for appreciating the experience of change.

Do it, Feel it,
BE it.

BE a hArtful Leader

Similar to coaching, you can't lead what you don't experience, commit to, or apply. As effective leaders, it's vital to stay consciously connected to the experience of leading and being led.

Stay connected to the experiences you have in being led and bring your conscious awareness to the do's and don'ts that support your leadership desired state. Pay attention to the reactions and emotional responses you experience when being led, reinforcing the importance of humanity in leading others. And, commit to creating a culture, aligned with your values and pledge to lead hArtfully that brings congruence to your actions, interactions and way of BEING.

Be empathic. Bring an understanding to your consciousness of what others may be experiencing when stepping into spaces of vulnerability and uncomfortableness. And lead them forward, ever so encouragingly, engaging your heart and holding up the mirror to the courage and curiosity they have tapped into, daring to achieve a new potential.

Experience is an invitation to apply these practices each day, in every aspect of your life, discovering and reflecting on the positive impact you have in leading hArtfully, and noticing how your way of BEING is aligned with your purpose in wanting to lead others forward to discover their best selves, and what is possible in doing so.

Create an E-Tention to 'Experience'

... committing to doing, feeling, and BEING a hArtful leader each day, discovering your best self and the best in others.

Excite With Enthusiasm

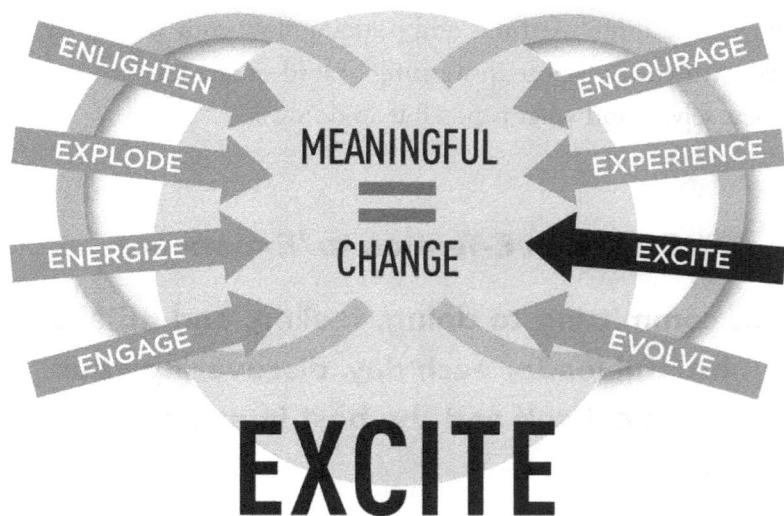

When I think about enthusiasm, there is a pretty clear picture of what that looks like. Zest, zeal, delight, and joy all come quickly to mind. Images of people with smiles the size of Albuquerque, with their arms raised to the skies, while dancing in place exclaiming 'Yes!' flash, imaginatively in front of my eyes; their positive energy bold, and unmistakably present.

Thinking about this in the context of leadership, it's equally possible to imagine what it might look like when a leader shares with their staff an observation and acknowledgement laced with enthusiasm: They approach the individual with a smile that stretches from ear to ear. Their energy has an aura that creates a force field of positivity. The anticipation of the leader wanting to speak positively is palpable. And, as they begin, their tone of voice is elevated and filled with excitement, with their eyes brilliantly communicating the sincerity of their words, revealing pride, delight, appreciation and achievement.

It's safe to say that many individuals have a clear sense of what 'Excite with enthusiasm' is and how this might show up in the leader's way of BEING. Easy-peasy, right? Well almost. With respect to this 'E', 'Excite with Enthusiasm', as much as it is about *how* to bring this forward, the question of *when* is equally, if not more, important. The presence of this 'E' in 'how we show up' is deliberate and consistently woven across all interactions throughout the day.

Exciting with enthusiasm is not limited to the 'above and beyond' accomplishments made by your staff. Rather, they are those every day, routine actions that often go unnoticed, that have an exceptionally remarkable impact on the human experience. See the routine as remarkable and overcome an often underlying impediment in how we show up as leaders, to repeatedly excite with enthusiasm.

I recall a conversation with Sara, a new leader in an outpatient clinic, where we were discussing the benefits of holding up the mirror to positively reinforce performance. Her deep belief that people were hired and expected to accomplish their work responsibilities at a specific level of job performance, blocked her from appreciating and acknowledging the routine actions accomplished each day by her staff. Sara's mindset, and open acceptance of this rooted belief in expected behavior, made it difficult to adopt an enthusiastic energy.

See the routine as remarkable.

Her commitment, however, to an organizational desired state where her staff felt appreciated, valued and motivated to reach new levels of potential, opened the metaphorical door to exploring a new leadership way of BEING that included bringing enthusiasm into the everyday, expected actions, attitudes and behaviors of her staff.

Our coaching conversation began with peeling back the onion of assumptions to understand what was underneath her belief that only above-and-beyond accomplishments were worthy of recognition. Not surprisingly, this belief was grounded in a practice that dominated the belief and behaviors of past leaders whom she had worked for. When asked what new levels of performance might be possible if her observations and acknowledgements had no boundaries, the idea of limitless potential, beyond her own expectations came, ironically, to mind. Shattering Sara's assumptions and fixed beliefs unlocked the opportunity to explore a leadership practice and experience filled with enthusiasm.

Coaching conversations begin with peeling back the onion of assumptions.

Within the healthcare setting, introducing yourself, and communicating to the patient your role in their care, is a fundamental, expected standard of behavior. And it surprises me, still today, that this is not consistently practiced across all healthcare professionals. This routine action, and to be clear, effective communication skill was also viewed by Sara as expected and essential, making it a great starting point to adopt the practice of exciting with enthusiasm.

Spending time with Sara and observing her staff interact with patients, it was immediately evident that they were not only consistently and routinely introducing themselves, but doing so in a way that created a remarkable first impression. Confident in Sara's ability to turn her observer on, calibrated to discover the best, I asked her to describe what she noticed in the patients' verbal and non-verbal responses to these introductions. With a new, enlightened perspective, she vividly shared how these simple introductions, offered by her staff, set a positive tone for the interaction. It was evident to her that these routine introductions were the starting point of creating a therapeutic relationship, inviting the patient into the care experience, and respecting their desire to know the individuals integrally responsible for their health and well-being. Without the introduction, she also realized that the values of partnership and collaboration were beyond reach, making it almost impossible to offer a patient-centered care experience. Ever so enthusiastically, she had, in that moment, recognized the routine as remarkable.

Sara's observations and renewed awareness of the consistency with which her staff introduced themselves, not only validated her staff's adoption of this important communication skill, but, in witnessing the impact of this expected behavior, expanded her perspective of the impact these everyday actions hold in creating exceptional experiences. Not only did she realize the magnitude of their impact on the individual patient, she also saw how, when effectively and consistently executed, they were crucial enablers toward achieving the much larger organizational objectives associated with creating exceptional experiences for all patients.

Her enthusiasm in this realization was evident, almost giddy with excitement in appreciating a new pathway toward improvement. Of course, simply appreciating this new awareness was not enough. Being able to verbalize and positively acknowledge her observations and insights would be crucial in adopting a strengths-based approach to improved performance. Bringing clarity to the importance of sharing her observations - with enthusiasm - was central to choosing a new leadership way of BEING. And, visualizing herself bringing this 'E' to her staff interactions was essential in taking the next step: action.

Together, we explored where she was comfortable, confident and willing to adopt this approach to engaging her staff. We imagined possibilities and planned for challenges. We crafted conversation starters and practiced their delivery. Key to all of this, was her desire to bring enthusiasm to her staff interactions in a way that felt authentic and natural. Over time, her enthusiasm, visibly cheerful and appreciative, leaked into her acknowledgements. And her staff responded enthusiastically, reciprocating with thankyou's and sharing their smiles - how you show up is how they show up. Her practice of exciting with enthusiasm soon began to grow - oozing into other routine actions, and bringing a remarkable energy of joy, connection and purpose in coming to work across the department.

Create an E-Tention to 'Excite with Enthusiasm'

... seeing the routine as remarkable and bringing joy to the work environment.

Evolve - Learn, Choose, Do, Reflect

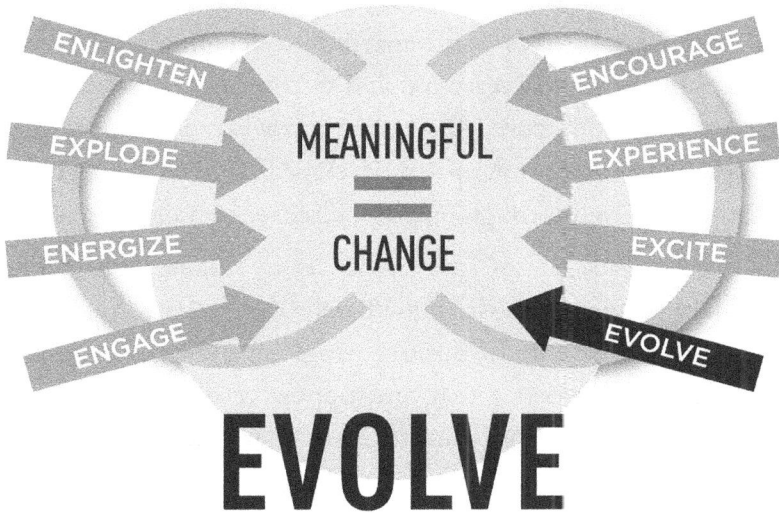

"This is a journey of discovery,
you get out of it what you put into it."

- DIANE ROGERS

'Evolve' is the last of the E's, and is the 'E' that ties a lovely bow around this notion of engaging individuals into meaningful change. Each of the E's is an essential element of how you show up as a hArtful leader. Bringing these leader actions, attitudes and behaviors forward, operationalizing them, and adopting them as your default leadership practices is, quite frankly, the essence of the purpose within this book - to evolve into a leadership way of BEING that discovers the best in others and cultivates a culture where new levels of performance and potential, fortified with fulfillment, appreciation, and well-BEING are realized.

The use of the word 'evolve' is intentional. Leading hArtfully is a journey of discovery. And underscoring this as an evolutionary journey is important to acknowledge. The change journey takes time. And changes in your actions, attitudes and behaviors, developing and using your strengths, turning your observer on and discovering the best in people is not a 'once and done' action. But rather, one where your individual way of BEING - how you show up - is developed, cultivated, nurtured and continuously evolved through practice, discovery, and reflection.

When I think about the word 'evolve' and this theme of evolutionary change, almost immediately there is a sense of growth and forward movement. Evolution brings images of change and the adoption of characteristics that are supportive of new environments and circumstances. 'Evolve' almost insists that where you are today is not where you will be tomorrow.

Evolutionary change is steeped with growth, development, progress, and advancement; unlike sustained change, which essentially means maintaining an achieved practice or improvement. And, when presented together, 'sustained change' is very clearly an oxymoron, making me wonder why leaders consistently limit performance expectations to sustainment. Countless times, I have presented change initiatives or improvement programs to organizational C-Suite executives, and each time, after laying out the plan, the expected outcomes, and the approach, I am asked, "And, what is your plan to sustain this?"

I almost giggle at the ridiculousness of this question for a couple of reasons. The first thought, of course, that flies through my head is always - 'Don't they get it? THEY LEAD change (not me). Organizational leaders are the individuals responsible to (1) Set the change agenda, (2) Build the case for change, (3) Develop and engage stakeholders, (4) Enable and equip individuals within the organization, and (5) Manage and measure progress and performance. And without their leadership and continuous communication of each of the organizational change elements outlined above, the change or improvement initiative will fail.

Leaders are also the individuals chartered to grow, develop and advance the organization forward. And so, sustaining any change initiative is not enough. Discovering ways to move beyond the current state and further into a new desired state - growing, developing and advancing - is evolutionary. And it is this practice of evolutionary growth that continues to move the organization and those individuals within it to new, undiscovered, levels of potential and performance. Evolutionary change moves us further into a greater, yet to be realized, new potential.

With this in mind, and with respect to how we are showing up as leaders to engage our staff and to influence and lead change, this 'E', 'Evolve', is focused on establishing a process to evolve your leadership actions, attitudes and behaviors to reach new potentials through learning, choosing, doing and reflecting; continually growing your comfortableness, confidence and competence in new ways of leadership BEING and advancing forward further - over and over and over again and again.

LEARN

The 'Evolve' 'E' is where all of the E's are brought together. Throughout these chapters, we have explored this notion of 'how you show up is how they show up' to influence the interactions with patients, staff and colleagues, to influence the well-BEING of your staff, and to influence new levels of performance and potential. And, the 'E's of Engagement' - new leadership ways of doing and BEING that discover the best in others and engage them in the meaningful adoption of new actions, attitudes and behaviors - have been outlined to influence and cultivate patterns of behavior where exceptional experiences, interactions, and relationships occur.

At the end of each 'E' section, you were invited to create an E-Tention - a thoughtful intention that would spark action to bring each 'E' consistently into your leadership practices. Bravo to each of you that created those E-Tentions. I'm totally doing the happy dance! Your E-Tentions are indications of what you have *learned* and what knowledge and perspectives you have gained as a result of the content. In creating those E-Tentions, you were able to take the information, principles and practices presented and translate them into a conscious, intentional action that brings that 'E' to life. Well done! High Five! Yippee!

Many times, during my workshops or speaking engagements, I invite the participants to write one E-Tention on a postcard. I let them know that I will be collecting them and mailing them back to them - to remind them of their E-Tention, and to reinvigorate their focus on leading hArtfully. Reading their E-Tentions, I am so very often overwhelmingly 'E-mazed' at their thoughtfulness, and depth of their connection to this practice of discovering the best in others and their individual choices in adopting new leadership practices. I am often additionally surprised at the variety of E-Tentions, as it brings to light how each individual listens, learns and adopts new practices, personalizing the information in ways that work best for their individual work and life experiences. E-Tentions also highlight the uniqueness of each individual and validate my intention to create an experience that is meaningful to each individual, in whatever way they choose to participate and engage: Much like leading hArtfully - meeting individuals where they are at and trusting their capacity to do and BE their best. Here are but a few E-Tentions to spark your E-mazement at the possibilities.

Create an **E-tention**

— · — · — · — · — · — · —

- *I will turn my observer on… notice what my team is doing well… see their magnificence!*

- *I will energize with the possibility of a new way, helping staff to connect in a way that is meaningful to them. What we do matters!*

- *I will leave footprints that others will want to follow*

- *I will be the best version of myself as a leader by encouraging my staff to see their strengths and to help them remember what they do matters.*

- *I will hold up the mirror for others to see their strengths*

- *I will encourage everyone to see their best self… so we can change a world!*

- *How I show up is how they show up*

— · — · — · — · — · — · —

CHOOSE But simply having the knowledge of an 'E' - what you've learned - does not bring about a change in leadership practice or affect and influence the culture you wish to create. Consciously *choosing* to take action to adopt an 'E' is crucial to shifting your leadership practices, inviting individual engagement and meaningful change. Choice is taking the time to define, in detail, the desired state that an 'E' may bring, and identify the importance of this choice… to you. Change occurs when there is individual meaningfulness attached to it - the 'what's important about this to me' response. And without a clear understanding and definition of the importance, adopting new actions, attitudes and behaviors can easily fall in the 'too hard pile'. The meaningfulness of your desired state drives you forward and motivates you to move past the obstacles, challenges and rigid ways of thinking that get in the way of adopting new actions, attitudes and behaviors.

Choice includes bringing clarity and specificity to your E-tention; clarifying your response to the question of meaningfulness and what the desired state offers, and specifying what actions you will take to adopt a new way of leading. This is where the rubber meets the road. Without a choice to take action, there is little chance of evolutionary change. Choice is fundamental to engaging individuals in a change and sparked by conversation and powerful questions that invite thoughtfulness, discovery, reflection and action.

Choice is not an 'I'll do it' intention statement. Rather, choice is a well-defined vision of the E-tentional outcome, why it is important and what specific steps or actions are needed to achieve it. Here are some questions you can ask to bring clarity to a well-defined desired state.

- - · - · - · - · - · - · -

- *What is important to you about bringing that E into your leadership practices?*

- *What would your department look and feel like if this E were consistently present?*

- *What happens if you do not bring this E into your leadership practice?*

- *How does this E support your organizational goals and objectives?*

- *As you think about how you showed up, what would bringing this E into your leadership way of BEING offer you?*

- *What has kept you (and could continue to keep you) from bringing this E into your practice?*

- *What strengths, characteristics and/or qualities exist within you that you can leverage to bring this E into your practice?*

- - · - · - · - · - · - · -

Shifting from the 'I'll do it' intention statement to defined action steps, requires you to get into the details and bring granularity and specificity to what you will do and BE. It's not enough to simply say, for example, "I'll encourage at all levels", but rather to specify what 'encourage' actions, attitudes and behaviors might look like in how you show up.

— · — · — · — · — · — · — · —

- *What words will you adopt to encourage? Be specific.*

- *What actions will you look for in your staff to encourage? Be specific.*

- *How will you show up with an encouraging attitude? Be specific.*

- *How will you ensure that ALL individuals experience your encouragement? Be specific.*

- *What will you notice in your encouragements that will motivate you to continue? Be specific.*

- *How often will you bring the practice of encouragement to your practice? Be specific.*

- *What triggers, reminders, and/or prompts will you create to activate this intention into action? Be specific.*

— · — · — · — · — · — · — · —

'Evolve' is, perhaps, the most important 'E' in shifting how you choose to show up.

Already, I can hear you saying out loud that this is all getting in the 'too hard pile', and that taking the time to craft these responses - thoughtfully, and with the intention of bringing them forward - takes too much time (that you don't have) and is too much work. And yes, I suppose it does take effort and more time than simply making a declaration of change and hoping it happens - which is why 'Evolve' is, perhaps, the most important 'E' in shifting how you choose to show up. Bringing change to your leader practice boils down to choice. You have the ability to choose how you wish to move forward: What will you choose?

> *"Do. Or do not. There is no try."*
>
> - YODA, THE EMPIRE STRIKES BACK

DO

After making the choice to adopt an 'E' into your leadership practice, the next step is doing it. And while it sounds ever so simple in concept, adopting new actions, behaviors and ways of BEING into your everyday leader lives can be quite uncomfortable, difficult and challenging to build a productive habit. Consider a personal goal that you wanted to achieve - for example, losing 10 pounds, and the action you identified to do, to help achieve that goal was exercising 30 minutes every day. How successful were you in immediately building a habit of behaviors that supported your goal attainment? The truth is, kick-starting new behaviors and getting them to 'stick', to create effective patterns of behavior, can be challenging. In choosing to BE a hArtful leader, and in shifting from learning to doing, consider the following to support you further in creating a leadership practice that discovers the best in others.

Start Small - Identify 'one thing' you choose to bring forward further into your leadership practices. Do not jump fully into the deep end of change and choose to bring all of the E's into your practice at once. Pick one; and spend some time practicing that 'E', integrating your intentions into your day to day operational interactions. Break that 'E' into smaller, specific actions that bring you closer to your desired state.

For example, bringing 'Enlighten with Purpose' into your leader practices might be kick-started by opening a staff meeting with a conversation about why each individual went into healthcare, and what brings them joy. Be careful to bring your most authentic, curious self to the conversation, encouraging their choice to share, and acknowledging the strengths, characteristics and qualities present in their lived experiences. The information that you gather in hearing your staff's choices to do the important work of caring for others can then fuel other interactions with reinforcement and connection to purpose.

Set the Stage - Take the time to envision what an 'E' might look like in how you show up and within your interactions. Consider that your 'E' conversations and ways of BEING may also be new to your staff. Bringing your strength of honesty forward to create a transparent, authentic dialogue is important to consider. Setting the stage includes imagining the responses from your staff - both verbal and non-verbal - to guide your actions, attitudes and behaviors and to bring further clarity of proof of the presence of an 'E'.

Visualize, for example, how you might invite your staff into a conversation around purpose. Consider who might be present in a meeting where you introduce this conversation and, perhaps, give them a heads-up as to what you are wanting to do and why it's important to you as a leader of their team. Ask someone from the team if they would be willing to kick off the conversation. And, be prepared to lead the conversation by sharing your story of why you went into healthcare and what brings you joy… How you show up is how they show up.

How You Show Up Matters - How you choose to show up matters, and defining the experience you wish to create is essential to guide how you wish to be present. Ask yourself, 'What experience do I wish to create?' Imagine, as they are leaving the meeting or interaction, what you wish them to be feeling - uplifted? supported? encouraged? appreciated? Bring clarity, specificity and definition to the experience you wish to create, as it sets the intention, attitude and behaviors of how you show up. Not unlike establishing an agenda of objectives for a meeting or encounter, delineating what experience you wish to create is equally important in engaging individuals to move closer toward the desired state.

Consider what energy you will bring into the room. Will you arrive 'exploding with passion', cheerful and ready to hear - truly hear - their responses? Or will your energy, actions and attitude be unsure, hurried and noncommittal? What beliefs and/or assumptions (e.g., "People won't care", "They'll think this is stupid", "What good will this do?") do you hold, and choose to alter, that might get in the way of bringing an 'E' forward? What new possibilities might exist if each individual is open to sharing why they do what they do?

And when your staff chooses to step into this new space of vulnerability and courage, listen. Truly listen to their stories. Hear the significance of their lived experience in their words and tone of voice. Appreciate their willingness to bring a part of themselves to an atypical place of sharing. Consider what you want each individual to experience in creating and sharing these conversations; and what actions, attitudes and behavior you want to bring to how you show up to create that experience. Playing this experience tape forward helps guide your intentions and ways of BEING, creating a space for genuineness that conveys truth and authenticity.

Do Not Make it a 'Thing' - The biggest caution I would offer, in all of this, is: do not make any of the E's or leading hArtfully practices a 'thing'. 'Things' are not personal. Nor do 'things' suggest a connection to or caring for an individual. 'Things' are shortcuts to 'checking the box'. 'Things' do not invite authenticity. And 'things' bypass those fundamental essential behaviors that lead, inspire, and encourage others to create and reach new potentials. Leverage your strength of curiosity, honesty, kindness and trust to create an environment that invites conversation… about the individual. Pay attention to how the energy shifts in the room, bringing with it positive emotion, engagement, meaningfulness and accomplishment - elements and evidence of well-BEING.

To be clear, if you choose, for example, to bring 'Enlighten with Purpose' into your leader practices and your 'one thing' action is to explore why people went into healthcare, please do not start with a 'rule' to open every staff meeting with someone sharing their response to this new 'agenda item'. Doing so could compromise your intention and, quite possibly, move your team quickly from engaged to disengaged.

Be creative in your approach and trust your best self intentions to connect to the humanity within each of us. Prepare and practice. Get comfortable, confident and competent in your actions, attitudes and behaviors and then, just do it.

REFLECT Bringing the practice of reflection into your evolutionary journey of leading hArtfully is important to not only understand the impact (internally and externally) of your actions, but to integrate new ideas, thoughts and concepts into embedded habits of ways of doing and BEING. There is deliberateness and intentionality to a reflective practice, bringing thoughtful, conscious awareness and insight to and from your experience. Here are some questions you can ask yourself to prompt reflection.

— · — · — · — · — · — · — —

- *What happened when you brought this E into your practice?*
- *What made it easy / difficult to bring this E forward?*
- *What reactions did you notice in others?*
- *What strengths did you leverage within yourself that supported your adoption of this E?*
- *What did you learn in stepping into a new way of Doing / BEING?*
- *What did you notice that excited you?*
- *What did you notice that opened up your mind to new possibilities when bringing this E forward further into your leadership practices?*

— · — · — · — · — · — · — —

Reflective practice opens the space for exploration that, through insight, awareness, clarity and meaning, amplifies our motivation and commitment toward the desired state. Dr. Anderson, an orthopedic surgeon, brought this idea of motivation and commitment forward, ever so eloquently in a follow-up coaching conversation one afternoon. Her words underscored what happens when the journey of discovery is important enough to do the work. She was tired that day, having seen more than fifty patients, and I recall mentally noting her continued commitment and choice to attend our coaching sessions.

Through our conversation, and within her own discoveries and reflections, she had outlined several actions she wanted to bring forward further into her leadership practice and patient interactions. Almost immediately, after declaring them out loud, she looked at me thoughtfully and then said - "I didn't expect to have to do this much work." I asked her what she meant by her statement; to which she explained, she thought I, as a coach, would be making suggestions and recommendations for her to adopt, versus the client uncovering, through her own discovery and reflection, prompted through my questions, actions that *she* would choose to take to move closer to her desired state. Her statement was a validation of her efforts. And I could hear in her voice a sense of accomplishment. She acknowledged the value and importance of reflections, in particular, echoing the power of my questions in generating meaningful motivation and bolstering her comfortableness, confidence and competence to make the shift from where she was to where she wanted to be.

Each of the elements of Evolve - Learn, Choose, Do and Reflect are imperative to creating leadership pathways that engage, encourage and excite individuals to be their best selves, strengthening actions, attitudes and behaviors that foster new levels of performance and individual well-Being.

Create an E-Tention to 'Evolve'

... stepping into the space of Learning, Choosing, Doing and Reflecting, and embarking on a journey to discover the best in others.

The Ease of Leading hArtfully

$$E's = mC^2$$

Engagement = meaningful Contagious Change

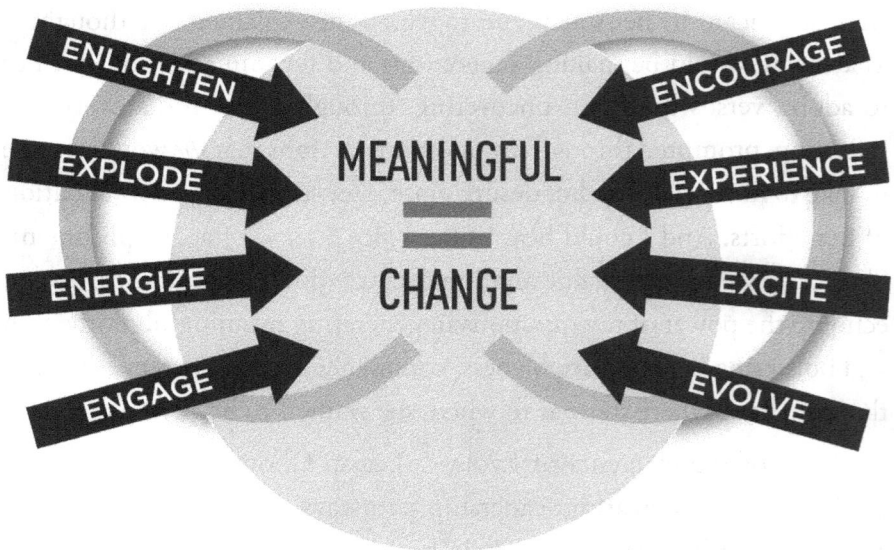

The ease of leading hArtfully occurs when you bring 'The E's' into your leadership practices comfortably, confidently, and competently. Connecting with, and discovering the magnificence in, each individual takes practice and is an evolutionary change. Finding your way forward, and being comfortable with new actions, attitudes and behaviors, creating new conversations, and consciously leveraging your strengths, characteristics and qualities to discover the best in others takes time. Turning your observer on and paying attention to the progress toward your desired state, shifts in performance and the positive impact on your well-BEING will continue to fuel your energy of effort.

What follows is a summary of the E-tention invitations to support your journey of discovery and guide your E-tentions toward meaningful contagious change.

Enlighten with Purpose - Create an E-tention to 'Enlighten with Purpose', bringing questions that create meaningful conversations, connected to purpose, to your interactions.

Bring definition and understanding to what is behind your desire to adopt this new way of leading. Create practices aligned with your authentic self. Bring congruence to the values you hold in how you want to connect and be with individuals. Connect further to your purpose and what is meaningful to you as a leader. Let go of any 'pre-determined' norms of a 'command and control' leadership style, and explore what resonates with you with an enlightened sense of purpose in leading hArtfully.

Explode with Passion - Create an E-Tention to 'Explode with Passion', leaving footprints that others will want to follow.

Find the space where you have more energy. Bring your passion forward in your verbal and nonverbal communications. Connect to your passion for making a difference and bringing what matters to you forward in your actions and interactions. Feed the energy behind your passion that fuels a leading hArfully way of BEING forward.

Energize with the Possibility of a New Way - Create an E-Tention to 'Energize with the Possibility of a New Way', bringing awareness to what is meaningful, impactful and possible when new ways of doing and BEING are attempted.

Calibrate your observations and awareness to notice new ways of doing and BEING. Pay attention to what possibilities you have created - in your relationships, within your environment, within yourself, as a result of your choice to lead hArtfully. Bring clarity to your actions and strengths that have been leveraged forward further. Foster a practice of acknowledging yourself, holding up the mirror to new actions and strengths that you have chosen to bring forward. Correlate the experience created by the actions, attitudes and behaviors you have chosen to adopt and that energize your next steps forward.

Engage the Heart - Create an E-Tention to 'Engage the Heart', BEING your best self to discover the best in others.

Connect with individuals at the heart level. Access your superpower to make people un-invisible. See the humanness in each individual and bring your caring best self forward, letting them know they matter. Change your conversations to engage the heart, connecting your actions, attitudes and behaviors to what matters most - each other. Notice what you experience, what positive emotions and levels of fulfillment you experience in leading through your heart.

Encourage at All Levels - Create an E-Tention to 'Encourage at All Levels', creating conversations that feed forward, fostering new levels of potential and well-BEING in everyone.

Turn your observer on and calibrate it to notice the magnificence within each individual. Set aside those 'shoulds' and 'shouldn'ts' that get in the way of offering unconditional positive regard. Shift your mindset to open the space to believe that each individual has within themselves the capacity to do and BE their best. Alter your leader practices from giving feedback to feeding forward, creating conversations that nurture and feed individuals with fuel that catapults them to the next level of performance.

Experience it - Do it, Feel it, BE it - Create an E-Tention to 'Experience', committing to doing, feeling and BEING a hArtful leader each day, discovering your best self and the best in others.

Do it, feel it, BE it. Stay consciously connected to the experience of leading and being led. Commit to creating a culture aligned with your values and one that holds up the mirror to the magnificence present in each individual. Be empathic. Show up each day consciously and intentionally to BE your best self and to discover and acknowledge the best in others.

Excite with Enthusiasm - Create an E-Tention to 'Excite with Enthusiasm', seeing the routine as remarkable and bringing joy to the work environment.

See the extraordinary in the ordinary. Pay attention to how the routine everyday actions, attitudes and behaviors present in day-to-day operations create remarkable experiences. Verbalize and acknowledge the seemingly insignificant, in ways that create OMG½(!) reactions. Adopt a way of BEING that invites purpose and joy into the work environment, creating the capacity to continuously change a world.

Evolve - Create an E-Tention to 'Evolve', stepping into the space of Learning, Choosing, Doing and Reflecting, embarking on a journey to discover the best in others.

BE your best self to
discover the best in others.

Acknowledge that bringing new practices into your leadership way of BEING is an evolutionary journey. Bring the E's forward thoughtfully and intentionally with ease, unlocking your process of learning, choosing, doing and reflecting. Increase your comfortableness, confidence and competence through practice, developing consistent, effective and impactful patterns of behavior. Bring clarity and specificity to your actions, attitudes and behaviors. Create E-tentions. Start small. Set the stage. Be intentional in how you choose to show up. Do not make this important work of leading hArtfully a 'thing'. BE your best self to discover the best in others.

VII
COACHING AS A LEADER COMPETENCY

"Create the space… When you take away the space, you take away the choice. When you take away the choice, you take away the learning. When you take away the learning, you take away growth."

-Marcus Buckingham

Coaching Is and Isn't

Coaching is a leader competency that supports how we show up to discover the best in others.

Coaching is a leader competency that additionally supports how we show up to discover the best in others. It is a leader practice that, when adopted, has the ability to improve performance, achieve organizational objectives and influence the well-BEING of those we lead.

Coaching is a scientific process that, through conversation and questions, helps the individual to shift from where they are - the current state, to where they want to go - the desired state. It is a leader competency essential to build trust and increase individual and organizational potential and performance.

> Coaching is NOT
> giving feedback, teaching
> or telling.

Coaching is NOT giving feedback, teaching or telling your staff how to do things differently. And, coaching is not a one-way directive specifying what should be done differently. I sometimes joke that leaders often interpret coaching as 'telling people to do things differently with a smile'. 'Telling' is not part of the coaching equation... ever.

Creating Meaningful Conversations

Coaching conversations are premised on the fact that, within each individual, they have the capacity to access their intrinsic strengths and motivations to bring about a change that is desirable to them. It is through the awareness that the conversations bring, connected to what is meaningful to them about their desired state and a strong trust in self, that leads to new and expanded choices, new possibilities and action - a shift from the current state to the desired state.

"Coaching is the art of creating an environment, through conversation and a way of being, that facilitates the process by which a person can move towards desired results in a fulfilling manner. It requires an essential ingredient that cannot be taught; caring not only for external results but for the person being coached."

-TIMOTHY GALLWEY

Coaching conversations create an environment of trust, meaningful relationships and encouragement. They are a two-way dialogue, facilitated through powerful questions, that uncover and discover strengths and capabilities that enable the individual to move toward their desired state. The essential ingredient - 'caring for the person being coached' - is vital to the relationship and coaching process. As coaches, we are trained to honor the belief that each individual is *creative, resourceful and whole*, and that each individual has within themselves the capacity to do and be their best. Vital to building trust, coaches bring authenticity to the relationship, where the client understands fully that we want what's best for them and that *they* are the experts in their lives. Reinforcing their intrinsic strengths, characteristics and qualities bolsters their trust and confidence in themselves to reach their desired state, appreciating their capacity to move magnificently toward their intentions.

Coaching conversations are not happenstance nor unfocused. Rather, they are structured in a way to consistently facilitate the discovery of what might be possible; prompting reflection, through questions that connect to meaningfulness and importance in reaching the desired state; and solidifying a new way of BEING by defining specific actions.

Coaching is conversational, grounded in trust and deeply supportive of the individual's desire to achieve a new potential, and appreciates their most remarkable strengths and qualities as a human being.

For some, I imagine, this notion of consistently creating conversations and discovering the best in people could seem a bit overwhelming, and even challenging in a work environment and organizational culture where time is precious, and old, authoritarian leader practices have dominated as effective in improving performance and achieving business objectives. That said, if there is the slightest bit of further interest in creating an environment where your staff feel confident, productive and valuable; where they are engaged in the work that they do because it matters to them, and where well-BEING is enhanced through increased positive emotion, healthier relationships, and a sense of accomplishment, then integrating a strengths-based coaching practice into your staff interactions might prove productive and helpful. And it begins with having a structure or construct that helps to create meaningful conversations.

> Coaching is conversational,
> grounded in trust and deeply
> supportive of the individual's
> desire to achieve a new potential.

ADRA Conversation Structure - Acknowledge, Discover, Reflect, Act

Coaching is a scientific process and an art that, for me, has taken years of practice and one that continues to evolve and grow. Over time, I have been able to genuinely and fluidly integrate into my interactions a dialogue that acknowledges the best in others, facilitates discovery and invites reflection to guide and specify next-step actions that bring individuals closer toward what is important to them. My conversations are generally always positive... and productive! Bringing a coaching competency into my leadership way of BEING was an intentional journey for me and one where, today, I fully realized that I could lead through my heart and at the same time be recognized as an effective leader.

This was an important realization and motivation to continue to evolve my leader practice. The greatest gift I received on this journey was that it was possible for me to show up each day as my best, most loving self, to support individuals in their work and development and be fulfilled; knowing that my actions, attitude and behaviors were aligned and congruent with what I valued - trust, love and kindness.

Developing coaching as a leader competency is an invitation toward fulfillment and begins with creating meaningful, person-centric conversations. ADRA is a defined conversation structure that I developed to guide leaders in bringing acknowledgements, discovery, reflection and action into the dialogue, each of which is valuable and supportive of a shift toward desired results.

The ADRA Conversation Structure enables a consistent approach to creating conversations that foster individual awareness, expanded choices and trust, and maintain the integrity of a strengths-based coaching practice. This structure guides the leader to acknowledge strengths, facilitate discovery, invite reflection and identify actions that move the individual closer to their desired state within each conversation.

ADRA is a defined conversation structure to bring acknowledgements, discovery, reflection and action into the dialogue.

Adopting the ADRA Conversation Structure, the leader begins the conversation listening with the intention to offer *Acknowledgements*, holding up the mirror to individual strengths, actions taken, and shifts in mindset, to name a few. Then together, the individual and leader explore what happened, what didn't happen and what could happen, *facilitating discovery* of the progress made and possible steps forward. The leader invites *reflection*, uncovering awareness, assumptions and choices that promote or prohibit continued advancement toward the individuals' goals. New *actions* are identified and defined, by the individual, to continue moving further toward the desired state, bringing ownership, accountability and commitment to the process.

The ADRA structure is comprised of four elements within the coaching conversation - Acknowledge, Discover, Reflect, and Act. Each of the elements is brought to the conversation to facilitate forward movement toward the desired state. It is not necessary for these elements to be completed in serial fashion, nor are they a 'once & done' component of the conversation. Rather, each of the elements is brought to the conversation artfully and heartfully, in whatever order, and however many times evidenced by the presence and intention to support the client on *their* journey toward BEING their best self.

Most often, coaching conversations begin with identifying the client's purpose and objective of the conversation or coaching session. This practice values and underscores the principle that the client is the expert in determining what is best for them and respects the journey toward *their* desired state. Leaders, however, charged with specific performance requirements, will often need to set the objective of the conversation, and at the same time, demonstrate a coaching competency by BEING coach-like. Preparing for these leader-driven conversations, the leader contemplates what they wish to accomplish in the interaction, being specific in its purpose and at the same time mentally associating the dialogue with the organizational objectives. As a practice that values the individual and believes in their creativity and resourcefulness to do and be their best, an intention is also made to identify the individual's objectives, and gather their input to their desired state, inviting them to verbalize and make clear what *they* wish to accomplish in the conversation.

As part of the ADRA structure, the leader also creates an intention around what they want the individual to experience within the conversation - bringing clarity to and opening the space for that experience to be realized. This is a key step in defining how you show up, making sure to be conscious of the energy you bring into the room, the words you choose, and the conditions, attitudes (e.g., unconditional positive regard, empathy and trust) and ways of BEING you offer in leveraging their capacity to do and be their best.

What follows is an outline of the ADRA conversation structure to aid in your adoption and development of coaching as a hArtful leader competency.

Acknowledge

Begin each conversation with an acknowledgement.

Listen with the intention to hold up the mirror to their best selves, highlighting and leveraging strengths.

Creating conversations that energize the possibility of a new way begins with an acknowledgement, a conversation starter that prompts the discovery of possibility and capability toward the desired state.

An acknowledgement is not a compliment - rather, it is a statement that brings consciousness and voice to an action, behavior, strength or characteristic that an individual has taken or used in support of their goals.

Committed to a strengths-based approach to change, you have 'turned your observer on' to notice those actions and strengths that were present, and are prepared to share your observations with the individual, taking time to bring details, clarity and specificity to what occurred and the positive impact that followed.

As you are sharing this acknowledgement, you are additionally paying attention to how you have chosen to show up, making sure the acknowledgement is genuine and encouraging. 'Caring for the individual' is present in your words and tone of voice, bringing an authentic interest and enthusiasm to your acknowledgement. Making a connection between their actions and behaviors encourages an ongoing awareness of their progress in moving toward their desired state.

Oftentimes, I will begin a coaching conversation with an invitation to the client to share something they would like to acknowledge themselves for as a step they took toward their desired state. I might say - 'tell me something you want to acknowledge yourself for this week'. This invites them fully into the conversation and reinforces their accountability toward their capacity to do and BE their best. As they share, I am listening with the intention to hold up the mirror to their best selves, to reflect back what I heard, being specific to highlight and bring conscious awareness to their strengths and capabilities that contributed to that new action, attitude or behavior.

Listen with the intention to hold up the mirror to their best selves.

So, what on earth might an acknowledgment sound like? It's really quite simple and unpretentious. Sit for a moment and think about an individual on your team. Picture them in any situation - meeting, patient interaction, colleague interaction, working at their desk intently on a project, walking down the hall. Now, turn your observer on and calibrate it to notice their actions, behaviors, strengths and qualities that were positive and productive? Let's now examine this a bit more fully, and imagine the person sitting at their desk, working intently on a project: what positive and productive actions, attitudes and behaviors could you notice? Their ability to focus and concentrate, for example, might be a productive quality that you observed in the way they weren't distracted by your presence. Perhaps, when you walked by, there seemed to be a palpable energy of creativity happening? It's possible you were struck by their ability to organize and dedicate the time to work on the project, given their busy weekly schedule and time-sensitive deliverables.

Let's pause here for a moment and recognize the potential for the presence of the old, default way of BEING creeping in, thinking that devoting time to the project is not an action that 'deserves' acknowledgement, as this is what they 'should' be doing. But, who made up that rule now made present through your own self-awareness and connection toward a new way of leading? Ask yourself what assumptions and attitudes are present that are getting in the way of creating a hArtful shift to bring 'encourage at all levels' into your intentions and conversation. Consider what might be possible in the environment that you wish to create; one that values individuals and positively reinforces behaviors that maximize organizational performance, if you were to see past the expected and acknowledge actions, attitudes, behaviors and strengths that moved you closer to the desired state.

Having now fully calibrated your observation to discover the best and chosen to lead hArtfully, your acknowledgment might sound like:

> *"The focus and time that you've devoted to this project, not to mention your creative energy that was palpable as I walked by, is very much appreciated and noticed. Thank you."*

Note that your acknowledgement is intentional to reinforce what you wish to see more of - focus, creativity, devotion and commitment. And in bringing awareness of these to the individual, setting the stage to create a conversation that leverages these areas of performance, you are adopting a strengths-based approach to leading improvement.

And in acknowledging their strengths, characteristics and qualities, you are helping to build their confidence and boost their feelings of valuableness and appreciation. These positive emotions enhance well-BEING. And so, in offering an acknowledgment, you are additionally creating a path toward enhanced well-BEING for your staff.

See the Routine as Remarkable!

Take a walk through your department. See the routine as remarkable. Turn your observer on to notice each individual. Pay attention to how they are choosing to show up. Calibrate your observer to notice something positive and productive. Leverage the Encourage 'E' - 'Encourage at all levels'. Set aside all judgement and assumptions. Notice the magnificence that each individual has within them. Discover the best in others. It's there. Make the choice to see it. Share your observation authentically with the individual. Bring your acknowledgement to their attention and help them to appreciate that what they routinely do each day is remarkable.

To be clear, an acknowledgement is not - 'great work today'. That statement holds no substance to the qualities of their magnificence, nor does it invite a conversation. Bring clarity and specificity to what you notice, connecting the dots to the positive resultant impact. Invite their reaction and reflection to what you have shared, and take note of your reaction in bringing your best leader self forward with a leading hArtfully way of BEING, energizing your motivations to promote the possibility of a new way.

Beginning and threading throughout your conversations with acknowledgements develops a relationship of trust and support. Holding up the mirror to an individual's best self is a skill that takes practice, and one that can certainly shift your leadership way of BEING to leading through your heart.

Discover

Facilitate discovery on the progress made and the next steps forward.

Bring a conscious awareness to the conversation, exploring what happened, what didn't and what's possible.

To discover something is not a passive act. Discovery is filled with action, opening the space to uncover, find, examine, question, and explore. There's even a bit of intrigue and curiosity associated with discovery, making the invitation to step into action more appealing.

With discovery, I imagine individuals thoughtfully contemplating and considering their thoughts and responses to questions, deliberately digging deep into their brains to uncover significance. There's a sort of magic to discovery; a zealous accomplishment that occurs after some level of effort and intentional exploration, as if to seek and find a treasure hidden from immediate sight.

Discovery is less likely to occur when the coach tells a client what they should be noticing or when a leader tells their staff what to do. In fact, when told, there may be an almost deflated, cheated feeling that is experienced, as if to 'give in' and not honor the capacity to uncover the unknown.

*"The only real voyage of discovery exists, not in
seeing new landscapes, but in having new eyes."*

- MARCEL PROUST

'Discover', as part of the ADRA conversation structure, is steeped with questions, facilitated by the leader, to guide the individual through the process of discovering the unknown and experiencing the magic of realizing their own capacity to find their way forward, leveraging their best-self strengths, characteristics and qualities, and moving closer to the desired state.

Within the ADRA structure, and in the context of creating conversations that shift toward a desired state or goal, the leader facilitates discovery on the progress made and next steps forward. Together, through a series of questions and responses, they explore what happened, what didn't, and what is possible. Questions to prompt discovery are provided below.

_ . _ . _ . _ . _ . _ . _ . _

- *What did you discover?*
- *What would be possible if...?*
- *What excites you about this?*
- *How did you approach this differently from other attempts?*
- *What are you doing that is standing in the way of moving closer to your desired state?*
- *What happens if you don't take this step?*
- *What surprised you?*
- *How could you use what you experienced and learned in other areas of performance?*
- *What happened when...?*

_ . _ . _ . _ . _ . _ . _ . _

Reflect

Invite reflection. Uncover awareness of strengths, assumptions and choices that promote and prohibit progress toward goals.

Create a conversation filled with intentional, intrinsic exploration and meaning.

Invite reflection. Reflection helps to make sense of what was discovered, enabling the individual to articulate what they learned and its meaningfulness toward their desired results. Reflections uncover awareness of strengths, assumptions and choices that promote and prohibit progress toward the desired state And they invite answers to what's important within the awareness of an experience, in the context of their discoveries and intentions.

As a leader competency, inviting a reflective practice facilitated through conversation and questions, expands the individual's self-awareness, drawing further attention to what's needed and what's important to change actions, attitudes and behaviors in support of desired results.

> Inviting a reflective practice facilitated through conversation and questions, expands the individual's self-awareness.

Built into the reflective practice is the continued commitment to learn and grow, without which, the response to the 'so what' question would be left unanswered and any motivation diminished. Consider these questions to prompt a reflective practice in a coaching conversation.

- - · - · - · - · - · - · - ·

- *What's important about this to you?*

- *Take a moment to 'look back': What do you notice?*

- *How does what happened support your desired state?*

- *What are you learning (... about yourself, about leadership, about your department)?*

- *What sense do you make of this?*

- *What do you find yourself managing / regulating?*

- *What has contributed to your progress?*

- *What was particularly challenging: What strengths did you leverage to overcome those challenges?*

- *What shifts in your energy, positive emotions, and actions are you noticing?*

- *What do you suppose is the greatest contributor to this shift?*

- - · - · - · - · - · - · - ·

Create the Space

Creating space for awareness, learning, choice and growth is fundamental to discovery and reflection. Space is open. It depicts images of a colorless vastness of emptiness in its description. Getting comfortable with silence and being silent is a coaching competency important to creating space. And trust within the relationship is the silent encourager that provokes thought, and fills the space with colorful, magical responses that, in hearing, you appreciate were accessed deep within this space of possibility. Giving each individual time and quiet to meander through the space of discovery and reflection is essential to invite awareness that fosters growth and potential.

Imagine yourself in a conversation with an individual, where you have thoughtfully and intentionally brought forward coaching competencies in your coach-like presence. Picture the individual thinking through your questions, uncovering meaning and significance within their responses. You are patient, attuned to their presence, and dancing in the moment with each of their responses, validating and encouraging continued discovery and reflection. Your conversation is fluid and natural. It is a dialogue, not a series of information-gathering questions, but rather a back and forth dance of awareness and meaningfulness. The intention is to trigger, 'out loud', the voice that prompts new insights and enlightenment. You are listening with the intention to hold up the mirror to their actions, attitudes and behaviors, as well as bringing a conscious awareness to their individual strengths, characteristics and qualities, connecting their discoveries, reflections and responses to their goals and desired state.

Act

Identify and define next-step actions, leveraging the insights made through discovery and reflection. Craft a conversation that brings ownership, accountability and commitment to the actions.

Act is the last element of the ADRA coaching conversation structure and one that is essential to facilitate change. Bringing the conversation to a place that specifies what actions the individual will take enables them to move forward further toward the desired state. It seems intuitive that defining and bringing clarity to the next-step actions would be naturally part of a conversation designed to create a change. Yet, it is so often easily 'forgotten' or omitted.

Giving voice to what next-step actions will be taken brings into the conversation clarity, accountability and commitment to the continued step toward the desired state. Having adopted a coach mindset of trusting that each individual has within them the creativity and capacity to do and BE their best, the conversation around action is created in a way that invites their ideas, plans and timing.

This invitation of ideas, plans and timing is prompted through the questions you are asking, taking note not to tell the individual what you think would be the best next steps forward. The questions that you are asking build from the acknowledgements, discoveries and reflections that have occurred earlier within your dialogue together. The actions that are identified and definitized, leverage *their* insights, and what they believe is possible to achieve and confidently attempt, bringing commitment and accountability to the individual's desire to reach a new potential.

Be thoughtful to continue to bring the ADRA structure within the action step - acknowledging their thoughtfulness and creativity, (among other strengths and characteristics). Continue to listen with the intention to hold up the mirror. Fluidly invite discovery and reflection around the actions they've defined, amplifying their connection and commitment to the desired state. Here are some questions you may wish to consider using as part of the Act step.

— · — · — · — · — · — · —

- *What next-step actions would you like to take to support this continued progress toward your desired state?*

- *What do you suppose might be the best first step to take?*

- *How do you see these actions supporting your (big) desired state?*

- *Would you be willing to outline an action plan with dates?*

- *How will you hold yourself accountable?*

— · — · — · — · — · — · —

Notice how these questions open up the dialogue for further exploration into understanding their level of comfortableness, confidence and competence in taking action - an important component to reaching accomplishment. Having the individual outline their actions honors them as the expert in their lives, strengthening the trust relationship and building in commitment and accountability.

To be clear, you are not inviting the individual to lay out their action plan, void of your input, recommendations or concurrence. These, too, are essential elements of the conversation, particularly one that impacts your individual and organization objectives. It is, however, the frame of intention, one that respects the individual and believes in their capabilities, that shifts the conversation from telling to co-creating. It is within this intentionality that a culture is cultivated where individuals feel valued, appreciated and encouraged to do and BE their best.

Having the individual outline
their actions honors them as the
expert in their lives.

Remember Russ?

Remember Russ? Let's explore how the ADRA conversation structure helped to energize Russ with the possibility of a new way. During our initial coaching conversation together, Russ shared what he wanted to see in his patient interactions, and what was important about that to him. In essence, through conversation, he brought clarity to what experience he wanted to create in his patient interactions. Providing excellent clinical care, of course, topped his list of objectives. Woven also into his description of the interaction were characteristics of how he wanted to show up to bring about an experience where the patient felt heard, cared for and validated. He described the desired-state encounter as one where he was present, bringing 'Russ' into the conversation, leveraging his unique, individual personal way of BEING - his humor, kindness, and inviting energy. It was important to him to be seen as comforting, unhurried, and a good listener; letting the patient share their 'story' without interruption. He also recognized that, to create a therapeutic relationship between him and the patient, it would be important to set aside any judgements and enter into the relationship with a 'clean slate'. He shared the importance of being empathic, as he wanted each of his patients to feel that he heard and understood the emotional message they were communicating.

Each element of the ADRA structure was present in our conversation, beginning with an acknowledgement of his intentional choice to create a patient interaction that was non-judgmental, empathic and supportive. Discovery occurred, not only in defining what attitudes and character strengths he wanted to bring into the room, but also what was required to trust himself to bring his best-self qualities into the interaction. Each component of the patient encounter was explored in detail, crafting images of what these qualities and characteristics looked like and how each of these was manifested through his actions, attitudes and behaviors.

Russ's reflections helped him to visualize and consider the possibility of leaving the emergency room each day filled with positive emotion and a sense of accomplishment in bringing forward new intentions and associated ways of BEING to his patient encounters. He outlined actions that would bring forward, and leverage, his individual strengths, creating a meaningful plan that would move him closer to the patient interaction he had imagined. With these in mind, he could now consciously and intentionally integrate these into his practice.

Our post-observation coaching conversations were equally important, as they would again invite acknowledgement, discovery, reflection and continued action. The ADRA structure was used to solidify the connection and understanding of strengths, choice and results. Acknowledging, out loud, and labeling what actions and attitudes he chose to bring into the encounter, and what individual characteristics and qualities were present, supported Russ's conscious awareness in how he 'made it happen'. Continuing the conversation to reflect on what he experienced in the interaction - energizing with the possibility of a new way - and connecting this experience to his desired state, helped to further make sense of the importance of bringing empathy, active listening and kindness more fully into his patient relationships. It was these structured conversations that led to his awareness, where he realized, not only his own capacity to change a world, but that he had a choice in each interaction of how he showed up to create and foster trusting, empathic, therapeutic relationships, letting the patient know that they mattered... to him.

VIII
HOLDING UP
THE MIRROR

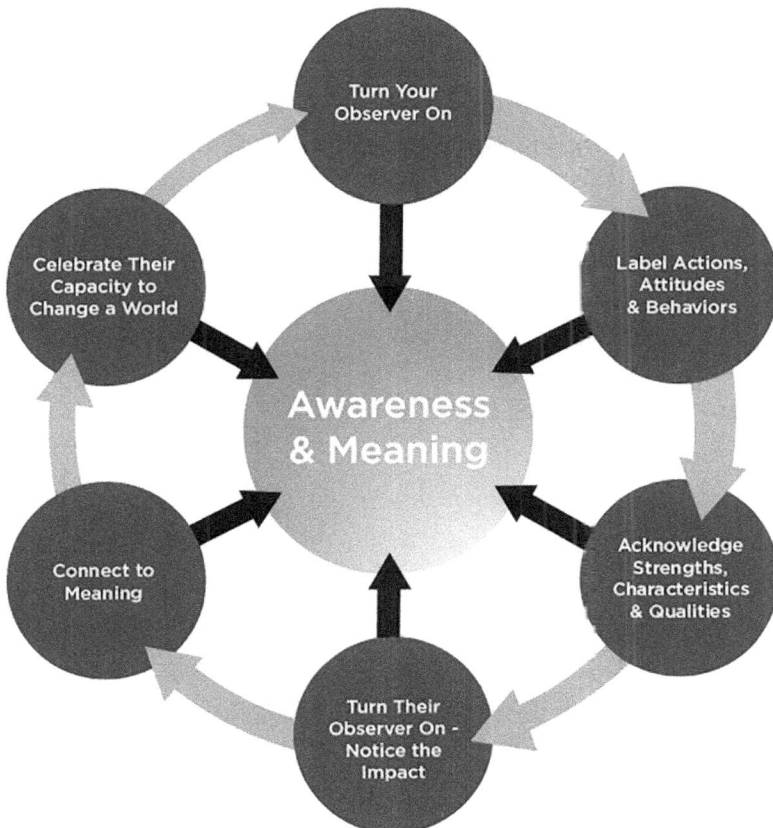

Threaded throughout this book is this concept of holding up the mirror to uncover the magnificence that exists in others, that when revealed, offers an unlimited resource of contagious actions, attitudes and behaviors to improve performance, enrich the experience and enhance well-BEING. In truth, holding up the mirror is not simply a concept, but rather a structured framework I developed that, when adopted in your leadership practice, brings clarity and specificity to the behavioral evidence of those individual actions, attitudes, strengths and qualities that positively impact the organizational strategic goals and cultural expectations. Holding up the mirror encourages repeatability, leveraging individual strengths, consciously, thoughtfully and intentionally to facilitate positive and productive change. Holding up the mirror is foundational to leading hArtfully, intertwined in the way you show up, and with the E's present in conversations that foster discovery, reflection and action.

> Holding up the mirror encourages repeatability, leveraging individual strengths, consciously, thoughtfully and intentionally to facilitate positive and productive change.

Before formally diving into the structure of the framework, imagine for a moment that you, again, are walking through the halls of your facility. Your observer is turned on, and intentionally calibrated to discover the best in each individual. Your energy is high, radiating outward, subtly adjusting the quality of your surroundings to friendly, inviting and reassuring. Your face is beaming with delight as you observe and listen to the interactions between your staff and patients. You are flawlessly familiar with the organizational language that describes desired actions, attitudes and behaviors and competently recognize and identify their presence. And, you are comfortable, confident and competent in sharing your observations and acknowledgements with individuals.

Imagined Interaction

Almost immediately, you hear a nurse enter a patient's room, greeting her with a *courteous, cheerful* 'hello' as she *refers to her by name*. You pause in the hallway, captivated by the conversation that continues. The nurse's tone of voice is *warm* and *pleasant*, and at the same time *confident* and *expert*. You can only assume that the patient has a worried expression on her face, as you hear the nurse's *empathic response*, letting the patient know she hears her worry and is there to help. She is *familiar with the patient's plan* of care and *shares the detailed information* with the patient, *explaining what to expect and why* it's important. She *invites input* from the patient and *validates her understanding*. You can hear the nurse say, "Does this sound like what you and your doctor agreed to earlier?" - reinforcing and *confirming their agreement* to the plan. It is evident that the patient and nurse are *collaborative partners,* working together toward the goals of the day. You notice that there is an ease to the conversation. It doesn't sound scripted or rushed. And you imagine the patient to be sitting up, appreciating the *patience* and *personalized caring energy* her nurse has chosen to bring into the room. And you are surprised at the emotional reaction you are experiencing - proud, pleased and profoundly aware of the impact this encounter has on the patient's healing. You smile as you move past the doorway, taking in the change-a-world moment that unfolded only minutes earlier.

Minutes later, the nurse walks out of the room. You approach her, your energy and BEING palpably positive. You smile, and she smiles back. She is familiar with what she anticipates will happen next, as you have made a consistent practice of holding up the mirror... sincerely, authentically and meaningfully. As you gather your thoughts, again you are surprised at the heightened emotional response you have, as you share with her each of the (italicized) elements that you observed in her patient interaction. You pause, letting the nurse take in your words and genuine acknowledgement. And, as you so often do, curious about her motivations and individual self-awareness, you create a conversation, asking her what she noticed and found meaningful in the interaction. You close the conversation, stating that you "imagine that the patient was thrilled to have her as her nurse!"

Deliberate, Appreciative, Strengths-Based Approach

Holding up the mirror is the ability to turn your observer on, calibrated to discover the best and acknowledge, through a strengths-based approach, leverage those actions, attitudes, strengths and qualities that cultivate and amplify a positive, productive, appreciative culture. The framework positively reinforces essential actions, attitudes and behaviors and highlights individual strengths that promote consistent, respectful, trusting, empathic, therapeutic encounters - nurturing and encouraging a pattern of individual and organizational behavior.

In consistently drawing attention to, labeling positive and productive actions and acknowledging unique individual strengths, holding up the mirror is a process that weaves into the fabric of the organizational culture behaviors that support relationships and interactions that promote personal, human and effective experiences for everyone.

The framework is deliberate; intended to be used consistently when meeting with direct reports, with employees, rounding on the floor, during staff huddles, or even within email responses, to discover the best in people; improving performance, enriching the experience and enhancing well-BEING.

Holding Up the Mirror - The Framework

Step 1 - Turn Your Observer On

Step 2 - Label Actions, Attitudes & Behaviors

Step 3 - Acknowledge Strengths, Characteristics & Qualities

Step 4 - Turn Their Observer On - Notice the Impact

Step 5 - Connect to Meaning

Step 6 - Celebrate Their Capacity to Change a World

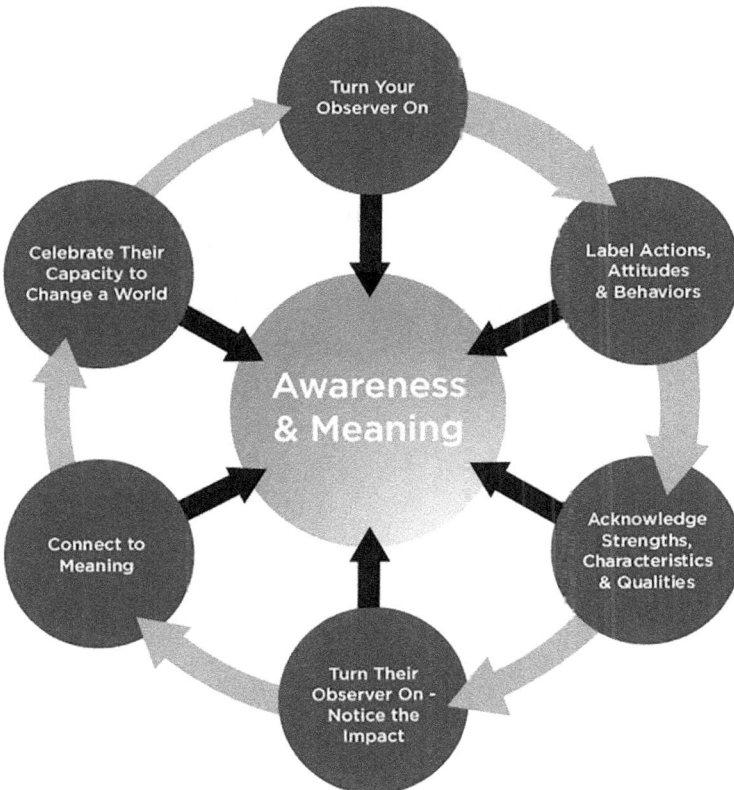

Step 1 - Turn Your Observer On

By now, you are familiar with the conscious intentionality there is in turning your observer on and calibrating it to discover the best in others. Within the Holding Up the Mirror framework, your observations are keyed to looking for specific actions and strengths. You have studied, and are prepared with mental pictures of what to look for. Flashcards of actions, attitudes and behaviors are streaming through your consciousness, easily recognizable and labeled with your observations. Filters have been added to your observer lens that draw your focus and attention to clearly see what is being done well and how it is BEING accomplished, helping to blur your previously default pattern of noticing 'opportunities' and 'issues'.

This is no easy task to shift your observations from seeing what's wrong to focusing on what's right. I get it... particularly at the beginning of bringing this into your leadership practice. But it is essential to lead hArtfully and to hold up the mirror to the magnificence that exists ever so prominently throughout your departments. Even still today, as I walk onto the floor, I consciously tune my observer to notice the best. The 'opportunities' - cleanliness, attentiveness, responsiveness, respectfulness (to name a few) - exist, for sure. But, I have witnessed, measured and reported, that in consistently holding up the mirror, the 'opportunities' grow far less, and cultures shift toward ones that are supportive, effective and productive in meeting the organizational objectives.

Step 2 - Label Actions, Attitudes & Behaviors

Crucial to this step is having a definition of the actions, attitudes and behaviors that are the expected standards and organizational norms within the culture and contribute to exceptional human experiences. Most often, these are tied to the organization's vision, mission and values, and represent what the individual is doing to manifest these in their patient, family and colleague interactions. Having a clear definition of what you are looking for, as well as a defined language or label that describes them consistently, is important to associate the action, attitude or behavior with the expected skill or standard, laying the foundation for conscious, intentional consistency in practice.

Taking a look at this in the context of the imagined interaction from earlier, elements of the interaction were labeled and italicized, indicating the associated communication skills (Reference Appendix A), patient-centered care standards and therapeutic relationship behaviors and attitudes present within the encounter:

- Courteous & Polite
- Refers to the Patient by Name
- Empathic response
- Familiar with Patient's History
- Information Sharing
- Explanations; What and Why
- Involves the Patient; Asks for Input
- Validates Understanding.
- Comes to Agreement
- Collaboration

Appreciating the importance of defining and identifying what actions, attitudes and behaviors you will intentionally look for, builds your level of comfortableness, confidence and competence in labeling them.

When I introduce the Holding Up the Mirror framework to leaders, I invite them to practice 'labeling' throughout the day in all sorts of situations and encounters. I suggest that they turn their observer on when they go to the grocery store, and listen, for example, how they are greeted by the person behind the deli counter - labeling the associated communication skill.

- Good afternoon, how can I help you? (Deli Counter Individual)
  - *Courteous & Polite - 'Good Afternoon'*
  - *Personalization - 'How can I help you?'*

When you go into the local coffee shop, notice how the barista welcomes you when you order your morning caffeine and identify the specific words that comprise the skill and/or action, attitude and behavior.

- Good Morning Diane. Shall we get your latte started? (Barista)
  - *Courteous & Polite - 'Good Morning'*
  - *Refers to Patient by Name - 'Diane'*
  - *Familiar with Patient History - '... get your latte...'*

Jumping back to the imagined interaction, and having labeled those behaviors present within the interaction, you translate your observations into an acknowledgment highlighting - Information Sharing, Explanation; What and Why, and Validating Understanding.

- - - - - - - - - - -

I can only imagine that the patient feels well informed about their plan of care today. Your explanation of what to expect was quite detailed. And I couldn't help but notice how you validated her understanding! That was engaging the patient at its finest! You were like a talking white board! You shared everything that the patient could expect to happen today.

- - - - - - - - - - -

Labeling actions, attitudes and behaviors positively reinforces what you want to see more of, cultivating a pattern of behavior focused on improved performance, and building confidence, appreciation and value within the workforce.

Step 3 - Acknowledge Strengths, Characteristics and Qualities

Acknowledge Strengths, Characteristics & Qualities

Within this step, the leader looks beyond what the individual is doing and into their BEING; those intrinsic strengths, characteristics and qualities that they hold within themselves and share with others. Again, the Holding Up the Mirror framework calls upon the leader to identify, by name, and bring visibility and attention to the significance of their unique individual, human characteristics.

Strengths, characteristics and qualities are those descriptors that describe the individual's way of BEING. Think, for example, of a very good friend. Picture this individual in your mind. How would you describe them? Imagine a situation or time that you were together. What qualities and characteristics stood out? Were they *kind, funny, friendly*? Were they *delightful* to be around? Did they have a *calm, reassuring* nature about them? Were they *confident?* When you are with them, what energy do you experience - *warm, caring, considerate?* How would you describe their spirit - *joyful, easy-go-lucky, happy?*

When you think about this person in the context of an interaction or how they approach tackling a work project, do you notice their character strength of *perseverance* present in the way they stick with the task through completion? Are they attuned to others' emotions and *socially intelligent?* Do they access their strength of *creativity* to solve complex problems? (Reference Appendix B, VIA Classification of Character Strengths and Virtues).

What about the presence of any leadership qualities identified in Chapter V - How You Show Up Matters? Are they *approachable?* Are they *confident* and *comfortable* in *making decisions*, effectively *engaging* and *guiding* others to follow?

Each of the italicized labels describe those unique strengths, characteristics and qualities present within the individual's BEING, bringing visibility to how they are choosing to show up. Holding up the mirror to an individual's strengths and qualities additionally helps to quiet the inner critic, bringing forward their best self, increasing their confidence and bolstering their way of BEING with magnificence.

Referring back again to our imagined interaction, those strengths, characteristics and qualities that were present, might be identified and labeled to include:

- Cheerful
- Warm
- Pleasant
- Confident
- Expert
- Patience
- Caring

Take a moment and consider how you might acknowledge those strengths, characteristics and qualities observed and heard from the nurse. Imagine that you are holding up a mirror and saying - 'Do you see what I just saw?' As you think about the imagined interaction, consider acknowledging the nurse as she walks out of the room saying…

— · — · — · — · — · — · —

"It is absolutely heartwarming to hear the cheerfulness and warmth in your voice when you are talking to your patients. I can only imagine that it helps them heal"

Or,

"WOW - you have such a way of bringing reassurance to the patient almost immediately with your confident and caring tone. Those two characteristics together are a formula for putting the patient at ease for sure!"

— · — · — · — · — · — · —

I'm trying to imagine your reaction as you read this. You might be saying - 'No way am I doing this. Those words don't even sound like me'. And, I suppose they don't. They are my words. But you can find words that do sound like you. Holding up the mirror is not intended to be a script for success. It is a genuine acknowledgment of an observation intended to bring visibility and awareness to the positive impact they make each day by reinforcing their best-self qualities. The intention in holding up the mirror is to magnify the essence of their best selves. Holding up the mirror is both leading through your heart - helping individuals to see their magnificence; and, from your head - describing and labeling your observations; to uncover the connection in how they are making a positive, productive, significant impact in the way they choose to show up. It is this level of clarity and consistency in these acknowledgements that help to build a practice of behavior that positively impacts performance and individual well-BEING.

Of note, holding up the mirror, turning your observer on and noticing what and how individuals are positively impacting the world around them is not limited to specific times you have dedicated to 'discovering their best self'. Remember - leading hArtfully is not a 'thing'. Rather, it is a way of leadership BEING, present in each of your interactions, whether spoken or written - it is how you are choosing to show up.

Not too long ago, I was on a video call with a colleague. After the call, I sent her an email that held up the mirror to the characteristics and qualities I noticed and experienced on the call with her. As you might expect, she was thrilled to have received it, validating the positive, contagious energy possible when choosing to discover the best in others.

I wanted to drop you a quick note to say how during the video conversation today I noticed the poise you had in being present. Your eye contact was impeccable, always looking at the camera (and therefore looking at me). Even your body language helped me to engage further in the conversation – crossing your fingers together, leaning in, nodding – communicated to me, consistently, that you were really present and listening.

—·—·—·—·—·—

I noticed also how it appeared to be a conscious action. This, of course, led me to think about what I look like on a video conversation. Oftentimes, I'm writing or taking notes – and while I'm present and engaged – for some reason, it appeared there was so much intention in your presence.

In any event – I wanted to say, not only how I appreciated that, but also how, in my own awareness, I may consider taking less notes and consciously, with great intention, look at the camera.

—·—·—·—·—·—

The invitation is clear - turn your observer on and discover the best in each individual. Bring clarity and specificity to those strengths, characteristics and qualities that are evident in their best selves. Hold up the mirror to their magnificence… and in doing so, notice your capacity to change a world.

Step 4 - Turn Their Observer On - Notice the Impact

Turn Their Observer On - Notice the Impact

Step 1 - Turn your observer on. Step 2 - Label what they are doing. Step 3 - Acknowledge who they are BEING. The next step brings visibility to what happened when they were doing and BEING their best selves. Holding up the mirror and bringing awareness to what happened as a result of their actions and strengths, connects the dots between doing, BEING and impact, tying the outcome to their specific actions and strengths.

'Energize with the possibility of a new way' is very much aligned with this step within the Holding Up the Mirror framework. By pointing out, with clarity and specificity, what happened, the leader is energizing the individual with what's possible for them to create. In other words, energizing the individual with the possibility of a new way of doing and BEING is the result of appreciating and understanding what happens when… Without an awareness of what happened, there is little connection to how individual actions and choices are significantly impactful. Nor is there any motivation to overcome the accompanying challenges and uncomfortableness necessary to bring new actions, attitudes and behaviors forward. Having an awareness of our best-self actions and strengths, and understanding the positive impact they have when accessed, can lead to an intentional practice of bringing those best qualities forward.

Energizing with the possibility of
a new way of doing and BEING
is the result of appreciating and
understanding what happens when ...

To bring 'what happened' into the conversation, you will once again turn your observer on to notice the impact. In this step, your observer is not focused on the best-self individual; rather, it is focused on the receiver of magnificence. You are paying attention to observe any verbal and non-verbal indicators of response. In this step, your observer is calibrated to notice the significance of what they did and who they were BEING. This step of the framework is not only essential to consciously and intellectually link behavior to outcomes, but it is the means to shift your conversation with staff from an operational and work focus to the individual, themselves. This step amplifies that their way of BEING, and the work they do, matters.

Linda works in Environmental Services at a hospital on one of the inpatient medical units, making sure the patient's room is clean, the trash is emptied, and the floors mopped. I met her one day as she was walking out of a patient's room, a gentleman who had been admitted a couple of days earlier. I had been standing next to his room, while I was waiting for a colleague. As she exited the patient's room, I immediately noticed her smile and positive energy. I introduced myself and said, "Hello." I started up the conversation, asking her what she did, and listened as she shared the details of her work responsibilities. But, as I hope you can certainly appreciate by now, I was less interested in the work itself, and more interested in the experience she was choosing to create with the patient.

Armed with my coaching competency and accessing my superpower to make people un-invisible, I asked - 'What's behind that big smile of yours'? Linda immediately lit up and began sharing with me how she loved visiting with this patient. She told me a bit about their conversations. Her animation and expressions, mixed with joy and laughter, made it clear that she not only genuinely cared about him, but that he too, enjoyed her company. She was, without a doubt, describing a change-a-world moment.

When she finished sharing, and using the framework as a guide, I shared with her what I heard, highlighting her choice to *make a connection and create a conversation* with him. I shared with her that I imagined how her *positive energy* and *brilliant smile* brighten his day. I let her know that I had heard *laughter* bellowing from his room, and imagined that he was ever so grateful that she was again assigned to clean his room, appreciating that it was her *delightful presence* that unquestionably impacted his day.

As I shared with her what I heard and observed, connecting her actions, behaviors, individual strengths and qualities to the positive impact they made to his day, I once again watched her light up. I could immediately appreciate that she understood that her visits with this patient were important, impactful and meaningful. Within this exchange between Linda and me, a change-a-world cycle was created - she had changed his world, and I was now changing hers.

Consider how your day might be filled, even overflowing, with positive energy, if there was a concentration of holding-up-the-mirror conversations with your staff, where you were helping them to see the positive impact they make each day - not only in the work they do, but in the way they choose to show up - their actions, attitudes, strengths, characteristics and qualities. Consider also, what might be possible when leading hArtfully, feeding your team of individuals with fuel that bolsters their confidence, develops their strengths and uncovers the possibilities in new ways of caring for patients and each other that exceed organizational performance expectations.

'Energizing with the possibility of a new way' is not limited to staff actions and strengths. It is likely also present within your awareness of the impact of your acknowledgements and capacity to change a world. Similar to the staff's experience in appreciating BEING their best self, you might also experience what it is like to BE and lead from a place connected to individual meaningfulness and positive impact. These palpable moments, when holding up the mirror, are snapshots of positive emotional connections experienced when leading from the hArt, caring for each individual at the heart level and discovering the best in others. And it is these connections that can encourage your leadership actions and behaviors to be repeated and practiced, fueling the contagiousness of this new way of leading.

> Holding up the mirror, not
> only brings the best of others
> into focus, it shines a light on
> your best leader self.

The duties that leaders have are often time-consuming, challenging, and exhausting. There is a plethora of operational and staffing challenges day in and day out. Leaders are held accountable for organizational metrics that have huge financial, clinical and operational impacts. The responsibility for patients and staff is heavy and sometimes burdensome. So, connecting to those moments, when you notice the depth and impact of your actions in bringing awareness to how another individual sees themselves, can be profoundly meaningful and important to *your* individual well-BEING and satisfaction. Holding up the mirror, not only brings the best of others into focus, it shines a light on your best leader self - guiding, developing, and piloting individuals purposely forward through their professional lives - unselfishly caring for and connecting to the humanity of this most magnificent work.

Step 5 - Connect to Meaning

Connect to Meaning

In my coach training, it was made clear, as a means toward change, that human beings, by nature, are in search of meaning... in the work we do, the relationships we build, and the choices we make. Exploring what is meaningful and purposeful is vital in motivating behavior change, as it is the oomph that propels individuals to overcome the impediments toward their desired state, and access the stamina to drive through the status quo force of complacency, uncomfortableness and safety.

Consider the context of a rather familiar imagined desired state - to be ten pounds thinner. There are multiple sensible reasons as to why one might want to lose weight and take action to reach this goal - improved health, feeling better, elevated self-esteem - but none, necessarily, strong enough to cause a sustained behavior change from the current state. Let's now suppose that your daughter is getting married. Playing the imaginary tape forward to the day of her wedding, imagine your family standing side by side together for the photo shoot. Imagine your daughter's smile and palpable joy she was experiencing on this most very special day. Visualize your presence, connecting and conversing with family and friends, many of whom you hadn't seen in years. And in each of those images, picture yourself looking fit, fantastic and fabulous! Hidden within these fantasies of fabulousness is the meaningfulness behind the motivation to adopt the new behaviors that would create the shift toward the desired state (i.e., lose those ten pounds). Exploring, through conversation, the 'What's' and How's of this new desired state, uncovers meaningfulness and purpose, giving voice and conscious motivation to new actions, attitudes and behaviors, overcoming the force of fixed practices and patterns.

Uncovering Meaning; questions such as those that follow allow you to explore the what's and how's of the desired state.

– . – . – . – . – . – . –

- *What's important about this to you?*
- *What would be possible if…?*
- *What's keeping you from…?*
- *What would be different?*
- *What will you notice along the way?*
- *How will this be different from other change attempts?*
- *How will you acknowledge yourself for progress?*
- *How will you find encouragement?*

– . – . – . – . – . – . –

Bringing clarity to your staff's actions, attitudes and behaviors and helping them to connect and uncover what is meaningful to them within your holding-up-the mirror conversations, not only helps individuals to consciously appreciate the motivation behind how they are choosing to 'show up', but is also associated with their degree of fulfillment and enhanced well-BEING. Martin Seligman, well known researcher, author and a leading authority in the field of positive psychology and wellbeing, describes in his book *Flourishing* the five elements of well-being; Positive Emotions, Engagement, Relationships, Meaning and Accomplishment (PERMA). Having meaning and a sense of purpose in what we are doing enhances well-BEING. He describes meaning as 'belonging to and serving something bigger than self', contributing to a sense of value and being worthwhile. In essence, well-BEING is associated with making sense of how what we do matters. Holding up the mirror and creating conversations that bring forward this connection to purpose and meaning invites fulfillment and well-BEING. And, so it's important… really important.

"Purpose is the deepest dimension within us - our central core or essence - where we have a profound sense of who we are, where we came from, and where we're going. Purpose is the quality we choose to shape our lives around. Purpose is a source of energy and direction."

- RICHARD LEIDER

One of the most profound coaching conversations I had, connecting meaning to what we do, was with Dr. Orson, a primary care physician. The conversation began by describing a patient encounter that he categorized as difficult and one where he was not his 'best'. In fact, it was an interaction in which he struggled to see how he made any positive impact in the patient's care, something very important to him in his work as a physician caregiver. He shared that the patient was reluctant, uninterested and almost defiant in not proceeding with a recommended plan of care. He additionally revealed that he felt it was a 'bad' encounter, having not successfully convinced the patient to fully adopt the proposed care plan. He described the patient as a middle-aged man, who upon entering the room was visibly and verbally filled with distrust and defensiveness. The gentleman was curt in his responses to the ubiquitous medical history assessment, making it even difficult for the physician to connect.

During our conversation, and within the exploration of the patient interaction, Dr. Orson shared with me the things he said, how he said them and the patient's response. His descriptions painted a picture of a caring physician, expert at what he did, and with a presence filled with patience, kindness, empathy and understanding. Within our conversation, filled with questions to uncover meaningfulness and purpose that stood alongside holding up the mirror to his strengths and actions, he began to realize how he offered the patient *unconditional positive regard*, and entered into the relationship with a *non-judgmental, respectful attitude*. Reinforced within my acknowledgments, he discovered his use of *personalization, repeating back the patient's words,* and *offering the patient alternatives* which, by his own admission seemed to support the patient productively and effectively. And holding up the mirror to his *empathic responses,* brought visibility to how he validated the patient's concerns, bringing forward further evidence of a two-way conversation that prompted engagement in a plan they were jointly creating. He shared that he wanted his patient to know that he understood his concerns and was there to help. At the end of our conversation, and in a very quiet, thoughtful, yet emotionally loud moment, he declared - 'I guess I really do make a difference'.

Step 5 - Connect to Meaning is a powerful tool within the Holding-Up-the-Mirror framework to uncover the presence of purpose, opening the door to fulfillment and appreciating how we make a difference each day.

Step 6 - Celebrate their Capacity to Change a World!

Our coaching conversation not only brought clarity to his actions and strengths that positively influenced the patient interaction, but additionally opened his awareness to consider a new perspective of how he defined a 'good' interaction. Holding up the mirror brought visibility to what was positive and productive within the entire interaction versus a much smaller view of success as measured by his expected outcome - agreeing to a defined plan of care. This new awareness expanded the choices he had in defining a 'good' interaction, bringing into play those characteristics of his best self that helped the patient to feel heard, understood and supported.

Seeing beyond his expected outcome and bringing awareness to those actions and strengths that were present within the middle of the interaction enabled an impassioned connection to what was meaningful to him in being a physician. Re-enlightened with purpose, he felt a profound impact from this new insight that day.

> *"What also fuels their passion for work is a larger sense of purpose or passion. Given the opportunity, people gravitate to what gives them meaning, to what engages them to the fullest commitment, talent, energy, and skills."*
>
> - Daniel Goleman

Holding up the mirror shines a light on the magnificence within each individual, helping them to see their capacity to change a world. It brings clarity and specificity to those actions, attitudes and behaviors they are choosing to bring into what they do. And by acknowledging these, you are positively reinforcing what you want to see more of, leading and guiding individuals forward toward new potentials, levels of engagement and well-BEING.

Holding up the mirror draws attention to their unique best selves, acknowledging and further encouraging the use and development of strengths, characteristics and qualities. It brings into focus that, in BEING their best self, they have the capacity to make a meaningful impact in the lives of others.

Holding up the mirror is a practice that, when adopted, has the additional ability to bring to *your* awareness your own capacity to change a world. It is this awareness and conscious intention toward a new leadership way of doing and BEING that lines the path of fulfillment and well-BEING. Positive emotional reactions, meaningful relationships and a sense of accomplishment are possible in your choice to discover the best in *you* as you lead hArtfully.

IX
LEADING hARTFULLY - BEING WELL

*"It's never about the end,
it's always about the middle."*

- DIANE ROGERS

It's Never About the End

This book is filled with stories, practices and approaches intended to invite curiosity and strengthen your commitment to artfully lead through your heart to discover the best in others. It further underscores that, in doing so, you have the ability to positively influence organizational performance objectives, and brings to light, that how you show up to lead truly matters to those you serve.

Yet, my primary reason in sharing all of this is not about the organizational and individual shifts that can occur. Rather, like so much of leading hArtfully, it is intended to bring a conscious awareness to what *you* experience when leading through the heart.

My Wish For You

My wish for you, as you embark on this journey of discovery, paying attention to the middle, is that *you* (re)discover your best individual and leader self. That you experience, deeply, *your* capacity to change a world, and that you notice the magnificence within yourself, present each day in your choice to bring your best self forward in how you show up on behalf of another human being.

I am in awe of each of you. You have chosen to explore a new pathway of leadership; one that offers days filled with joy and personal fulfillment. As you consider how you are choosing to show up, armed with the E's, and equipped to create conversations that discover the best in others, take notice of the positive, meaningful, personal experiences you create. Notice how what you do and who you choose to BE matters. It is the source of your individual well-BEING.

Take note of the personal, purposeful connection you have in leading others. Experience fully the presence of your passion. Be aware of your choice to connect at the heart level. And, in trying new approaches, find yourself energized with the possibility of a new way of BEING. Acknowledge the courage you had in encouraging each and every one of your staff and colleagues. And, in experiencing each new element of leading hArtfully, relish your excitement to bring an attitude of enthusiasm to each day. Honor this evolutionary journey, appreciating the growth that comes when stepping forward further into a new space.

And, as you choose to bring conversation to your interactions, notice how, in feeding forward your staff with evidence of their strengths and holding up the mirror to their best selves, you are changing a world... a world that has the capacity to create an energy of positive and contagious change, to do what matters most - being kind, and caring for others.

Hugs,

Appendix

Appendix A

Creating Meaningful Connections; Communication Skills / Techniques

Make a Connection

- Smiles

- Personalizes

- Eye Contact

- Touches

- Engaged / Active Listening

- Asks Permission

- Courteous / Polite

- Knocks prior to Entry / Sits Down

- Apologizes

Say 'Hello'

- Introductions - With Patient / Family
- Refers to Patient by Name
- Familiar with Patient History

Create the Conversation

- Creates / Continues the Conversation
- Does Not Interrupt
- Involves the Patient; Asking for Input
- Repeats Back Patient's Words
- Sets / Manages Expectations
- Explanation - What & Why
- Summarizes All Things Discussed
- Validates Understanding

Put at Ease

- Manages Pain
- Reassures
- Validates Patient Comments
- Empathetic
- Encourages
- Continuity of Care
- Manages Up

Say Good-Bye

- Comes to Agreement
- Offers Alternatives
- Turns Negatives into Positives
- Asks for Questions

Appendix B

VIA Classification of Character Strengths and Virtues

Character strengths are the core of who we are; the basic elements of our identity, helping individuals to function at their best. The VIA Classification offers a common language for describing good moral character and when used and developed contribute to well-BEING.

24 Character Strengths are mapped to six virtues; Wisdom, Courage, Humanity, Justice, Temperance and Transcendence

For more information on Character Strengths - www.viacharacter.org

Virtue of Wisdom

- Creativity: Original, adaptive, ingenuity, seeing and doing things in a different way

- Curiosity: Interest, novelty-seeking, exploration, openness to experience

- Judgment: Critical thinking, thinking through all sides, not jumping to conclusions

- Love of Learning: Mastering new skills and topics, systematically adding to knowledge

- Perspective: Wisdom, providing wise counsel, taking the big picture view

Virtue of Courage

- Bravery: Valor, not shrinking from threat or challenge, facing fears, speaking up for what's right

- Perseverance: Persistence, industry, finishing what one starts, overcoming obstacles

- Honesty: Authenticity, being true to oneself, sincerity without pretense, integrity

- Zest: Vitality, enthusiasm for life, vigor, energy, not doing things half-heartedly

Virtue of Humanity

- Love: Both loving and being loved, valuing close relations with others, genuine warmth

- Kindness: Generosity, nurturance, care, compassion, altruism, doing for others

- Social Intelligence: Aware of the motives and feelings of oneself and others, knows what makes others tick

Virtue of Justice

- Teamwork: Citizenship, social responsibility, loyalty, contributing to a group effort

- Fairness: Adhering to principles of justice, not allowing feelings to bias decisions about others

- Leadership: Organizing group activities to get things done, positively influencing others

Virtue of Temperance

- Forgiveness: Mercy, accepting others' shortcomings, giving people a second chance, letting go of hurt

- Humility: Modesty, letting one's accomplishments speak for themselves

- Prudence: Careful about one's choices, cautious, not taking undue risks

- Self-Regulation: Self-control, disciplined, managing impulses, emotions, and vices

Virtue of Transcendence

- Appreciation of Beauty & Excellence: Awe and wonder for beauty, admiration for skill and moral greatness

- Gratitude: Thankful for the good, expressing thanks, feeling blessed

- Hope: Optimism, positive future-mindedness, expecting the best & working to achieve it

- Humor: Playfulness, bringing smiles to others, lighthearted - seeing the lighter side

- Spirituality: Connecting with the sacred, purpose, meaning, faith, religiousness

WANT TO BRING LEADING hARTFULLY TO YOUR ORGANIZATION?

Connect with Diane!

Connect with Diane to explore how you can bring Leading hArtfully to your organization and achieve new levels of potential - together!

- Leadership Development - All Levels (Executive to Front Line); Individual and Group

- Professional Coaching - Leadership, Physician, Individual, Group / Team

- The hArt of Medicine® - Cultivating Experience Excellence through Engaging the hArt

- Experiential Learning Programs - Tailored to Strategic Objectives

- Team Building Retreats - Interactive, Inviting and Intention toward Change

- Keynote Speaking Engagements - Large and Small; Inspiring, Energizing and Motivating

- Cultural Transformation - Strategy and Implementation Planning; with Accountability

- Coach Development - Internal Coaching; Competency Development

Create A Conversation with Diane!

Learn more about the book:
www.contagiouschange.com/Keynotes&Books

Send an email:
diane@contagiouschange.com

@ Find and follow:

- **Twitter -**   https://twitter.com/contagiouschang
- **LinkedIn -** https://www.linkedin.com/in/dianemrogers/
- **Facebook -** https://www.facebook.com/ContagiousChange/

To order books in bulk: Send an email!
diane@contagiouschange.com

About the Author

Acclaimed leadership coach and consultant, Diane Rogers has a diverse background and a big heart, both of which power a simple and focused mission — to inspire individuals and organizations to harness the strengths and magnificence of people so, together, they can achieve higher levels of organizational performance and individual engagement. Founder and president of Contagious Change, LLC, Diane is best known for her breakthrough programs for healthcare organizations, where she has long been a trusted coach — sought after for her ability to inspire strengths-based leadership behaviors among medical professionals who want to optimize performance, experience, and engagement.

In a word, Diane's approach to leading and inspiring others is collaborative. In everything she does, she endeavors to leave her stakeholders feeling like their best selves — motivated and excited to engage and energize others. In a cluttered business marketplace of leadership coaches and consultants, Diane brings something refreshing and vital. She is more than a coach, a leadership consultant, and a quality and performance improvement expert; she is a masterful relationship builder who demonstrates, at every turn, the impact of bringing your best self forward in transformative ways to discover and leverage the best in others. Diane lights fires and changes the trajectories of careers and companies. She frees us from what was holding us back and points us — organizationally and individually — at a clear blue sky that is our new magnificent limit.

Diane is frequently called upon by leadership teams across various industries — including healthcare, technology, finance, and professional services — to do the important and deeply personal work of developing leaders, improving quality and performance, leading and implementing organizational change, and transforming workplace cultures. Diane's programs and approaches hinge upon her passion for hardwiring meaningful organizational change by equipping leaders to embrace her proprietary "E's of Individual Engagement" — whereby leaders learn to enlighten with purpose, explode with passion, energize with the possibility of a new way, engage the heart, encourage at all levels, experience more fully, excite with enthusiasm, and evolve into what she calls a "hArtful leader."

While Diane works with professionals in every sector, her programs and impact are legendary in the field of medicine. She developed The hArt of Medicine®, a program designed to engage healthcare professionals in creating therapeutic relationships and improving their communication skills through a unique experiential learning approach. Diane continues to work with some of the nation's top hospitals and academic medical centers. She also works with and supports The Beryl Institute, facilitating virtual classroom sessions, topic calls, and workshops. Diane is a Certified Patient Experience Professional (CPXP).

Diane has built her coaching and consulting practice upon a rich background, with a diverse history of demonstrated leadership positions across multiple industries, including healthcare, software IT, aerospace and nuclear power. As a professional coach, she holds PCC-level certification from the International Coaching Federation, as well as several certifications in positive psychology. Early in her career, Diane earned an undergraduate degree in mathematics from St. Louis

University and leadership certificates from the American Graduate School of International Management.

Diane's exquisite ability to help individuals and organizations hold up a proverbial mirror to reveal the unique strengths of every single person is more than just a feel-good exercise. "Holding up the mirror" — in organizations of all types and sizes — encourages repeatability of what's going well... leveraging individual strengths, consciously, thoughtfully, and intentionally to facilitate positive and productive change.

In addition to the leadership coaching and team development work that Diane conducts for clients, she also assists organizations with employee engagement initiatives, patient/human experience improvement, and more. Diane is a dynamic, energetic speaker who offers keynotes and presentations of all kinds, as well as summits, seminars, and group coaching.

Outside of her professional work, Diane is an avid runner and a glass jewelry artist. She lives in Mesa, Arizona.

Leading hArtfully: The Art of Leading Through Your Heart to Discover the Best in Others is Diane's first nonfiction business book.

www.ingramcontent.com/pod-product-compliance
Lightning Source LLC
Chambersburg PA
CBHW071601210326
41597CB00019B/3350